Money Honey

A Simple 7-Step Guide For Getting Your Financial $hit Together

DOWNLOAD THE BUDGETING
WORKSHEETS FOR FREE!

READ THIS FIRST

As a thank you for buying my book, I would like to give you the customized budgeting, savings, and net worth worksheets I've created 100% FREE!

TO DOWNLOAD GO TO:

http://eepurl.com/c1ro7H

FOLLOW ME ON SOCIAL MEDIA!

Facebook: www.facebook.com/moneyhoneyrachel

Instagram: @moneyhoneyrachel

TABLE OF CONTENTS

SECTION ONE: INTRODUCTION

Hello, It's Me

TL;DR Adulting is hard, especially when it comes to money management. With some sass and a little smartass, I'm here to make the journey to financial freedom easy and fun. After reading this book and learning the 7 Simple Steps, you'll finally have an easy-to-implement strategy that will help you gain control of your finances right away.

You know that feeling of not knowing what the hell you're doing? From dieting to salary negotiations to online dating, adulting is freakin' hard. For many people, money management is at the top of the list of Most Dreaded Topics Ever.

Not only is personal finance complex, but it's BORING. Ain't nobody got time for another dull, jargon-filled finance book. That's why I wrote *Money Honey*—to offer a simple, humorous alternative to the world of financial education. I'm here to turn your feelings of despair into feelings of enthusiasm and confidence so you can get your financial $hit together. And we're both going to have fun while doing so. Pinky promise.

I LOL'd at a meme I saw the other day that said, "I'm so glad I learned about parallelograms instead of how to do taxes. It's really come in handy this parallelogram season." Truer words have never been spoken. Unfortunately, the education system fails to teach us some of the most practical topics in real life, personal finance being one of them.

It's not uncommon for young professionals to have no clue how to manage their money. In fact, most people I know have barely mastered the basics of budgeting and saving, let alone the stock market. How can you learn when there is no formal education in place? Maybe your parents taught you a few tips and tricks, but not all children can rely on their parents to teach them about proper money management.

Not only is there a lapse in the education system regarding finance, it's not something you think about until you start making money. By the time you get into the real world, money management can be overwhelming. Suddenly, you are juggling 500 unknowns at once: Where do I get a job? How does health insurance work? Where do I get my suit tailored? Not to mention the financial unknowns: How much should I contribute to my retirement account? How much should I save? Should I pay off student loans or set money aside to buy a car? Many people are so stressed out by their finances that they shut down and ignore it altogether.

Millennials aren't the only ones who have unanswered questions—it's a tremendous percentage of the population. These people range from high school teenagers to some of the smartest, most successful people I know. I've helped hard-working stay-at-home moms, brilliant lawyers, struggling grad students, young professionals, and bright-eyed entrepreneurs. What do these people, you included, all have in common? You desperately *want to learn*; you are not content with staying uninformed. You are bothered by the fact that you don't understand finance and don't have a strategy. So, why don't you start learning?

The problem is that you don't know where to begin. (Or maybe you're so embarrassed at how little you know that you feel dumb asking.) You have questions about retirement accounts, student loan consolidation, mortgages, credit cards, and taxes; it's overwhelming. You may have asked family and friends for their advice or tried to do your own research, but in the end, those resources are either unqualified or boring.

Even outside of people you know and our friend Google, easy-to-understand and simultaneously engaging resources are not in abundance. Don't get me wrong; thousands of personal finance blogs, books, articles, and podcasts exist.

So, what's the big deal? Let's just say that it's hard to make finance simple, and most importantly, *fun*. As one of my friends said, "My boyfriend tries to explain this stuff to me, but my eyes glaze over almost immediately. The other day, I literally nodded off while he tried to teach me about mutual funds." The struggle is real, and that's why I wrote *Money Honey*.

So what do I know anyway?

My background is in finance. My obsession began in 6th grade when my parents enrolled me in a summer camp that required me to spend all day at a water park. 11-year-old me was horrified. A *water park*, how awful. To help pass the long and boring hours at the pool, I picked up a book called, "The Motley Fool Investment Guide for Teens: 8 Steps to Having More Than Your Parents Ever Dreamed Of." *Nice!* I happened upon this gem right when my intelligent parents began to teach my sisters and me about budgeting. One of my family's *favorite* acronyms was: NITB, which stands for Not In The Budget. (Right, Dad?!) The thought of having more money than my parents ever dreamed of was seductive.

One of the first chapters I read in the *Motley Fool* book on compound interest blew my mind. With the time advantage of being so young, I knew I could implement what I learned and be light years ahead of my peers. That book was a pure revelation. Even if you're not a teenager, I urge you to read it.

Studying my prized *Motley Fool Guide* at the water park sparked a frenzy that has lasted more than ten years. I've read every personal finance book I could get my hands on. I've learned about the basics like saving and budgeting and then graduated to the more complicated stuff like investing in the stock market. I went on to learn about how to create passive income, how to invest in real estate, and how to build my own businesses. By the time I was finishing high school, I had developed a mature and informed perspective on money.

The cost of getting a college degree terrified me. Because of what I'd learned about finances in my first 18 years of life, I was in a panic at the thought of going into debt for my education. Despite 99% of my fellow high school grads willingly taking on tens of thousands of dollars for their first *year* of undergrad, I was determined to not be like them. I understood a lot more than my friends did about the negative impact debt could have on my life. I made up my mind that I would not graduate with a single penny of student debt.

The summer before I started at Centre College, I happened upon a winning lottery ticket. This lotto ticket was in the form of a job offer from Cutco Cutlery, a direct sales company that sells knives. My mom was thrilled! (Not.) As sketchy as it sounded, I was beyond excited because I had never been introduced to a job where the harder you work, the more money you make. I sold $30,000 worth of knives that summer, set the record in Louisville, KY, and made five figures worth of cash. Combined with my hefty academic and piano scholarships, I was able to pay for my first year of college straight out of my own pocket. To this day, it's my proudest accomplishment.

At Centre College, I enrolled in as many economics and financial classes as possible and earned straight A's in all of them. I continued selling Cutco to pay for school. Three years later, I graduated with a Bachelor of Science in Financial Economics with, you guessed it, zero student debt. Plus, I had four job offers from various financial firms in Louisville. I began my post-college life as a licensed financial advisor at a large corporation. I've helped thousands of people get their finances in order and taught them where to put their money to get the biggest return on investment. I whipped each and every one of my clients into shape.

Since then, I've worked as a finance manager at a real estate investment firm and a financial analyst for a large manufacturing corporation. I'm currently an avid investor and business owner. No matter my job, I enthusiastically offer my financial advice to anyone who solicits it. I'm a personal finance geek in and out, so imparting my decades upon decades upon decades of wisdom (jk; only 2.5 decades) is nothing short of thrilling. My passion for helping others with their finances continues to be a driving force in my life.

Fast forward to today. Within a 24-hour span, I typically receive several inquiries from friends and family seeking out financial advice. My little sister relies on my help for budgeting, my parents for retirement planning, my older sister for IRAs and 401Ks, and my friends for anything from credit cards to student loans to investing in the stock market.

My peers constantly seek financial advice; this recurring theme tells me there is a problem in the United States: most people don't have a strategy when it comes to their money. And not only do they not have a strategy, but they don't know much about money management to begin with.

Luckily for you, this book will answer your burning money questions. Money Honey is a tough-love, need-to-know guide on all things personal finance. This $hit is too important to mumble and grumble about. From the people who suffer from falling asleep while attempting to learn about the stock market to those that cannot figure out how the eff taxes work, this book is for you.

Many will disagree. Maybe you think you don't need this book. Maybe you're in school, you recently graduated, or you just started your career. You have tons of time. Why bother right now? Why not enjoy life for a hot sec?

Because that's how bad habits form. Ignorance is bliss, but it's not good for your finances. If you don't realize how detrimental credit card debt can be to your livelihood, then what's stopping you from maxing out your credit limits? If you don't understand the importance of saving now, then where will you be in five years when you have no savings and a tremendous financial emergency?

Nothing—I repeat, nothing—is more important than learning the basics of managing your money. Starting right now. You literally cannot afford to put this off. Don't be like the millions of people that wish they knew all this ten years ago, or that have countless regrets on how they've used their money. Learn now so you can enjoy life later. I assure you: this book is for you.

This book is for the college student who is sick of feeling broke and wants to learn how to build up some savings. This book is for the young professional who has some cash saved but would love a strategy on where to put that money and how to invest it. This book is for the newly married couple that want to improve their credit while paying down their debt. This book is for the young mom and dad who want to save for a certain daughter or son's college education. This book is for any reader who wants to better herself financially.

With *Money Honey*, I have undertaken the unimaginable: making finance *easy* and *fun*. In the following pages, I will give you the need-to-know on all the basic financial topics. I cover a wide array of subjects because I leave out all the bull$hit and get straight to the point. You're welcome.

I'll start with the foundation:

- how to create a budget so you know where you stand today

- how to double your income and halve your expenses

- where to put your savings to get the highest rate of return

Then we'll move onto that bad boy called debt:

- how to lower your student loan interest rates via consolidation

- why credit cards are either your friend or your foe

- how mortgages work

- how to get a bombproof credit score

The next section (my favorite) is investing. Investing is scary for most newbies because it feels foreign. I'll walk you through *everything*:

- the difference between a stock, bond, mutual fund, and index fund, and which one is the real MVP for my fellow millennials

- how to put together an investment strategy that's right for you

- how to physically open up an account and make a trade, with screenshots included

- how retirement accounts work and when you should start saving for retirement (Hint: Now)

Lastly, I'll touch on taxes and insurance. You'll learn:

- why tax refunds should not be celebrated

- why long-term disability insurance is as important as life insurance

What's great about this book is that you can skip to the section you wish to learn more about. If you have questions on what kinds of stocks to invest in, go straight to Chapter 12. If you want to learn more about a tool for saving for your child's education, scoot on over to Chapter 6. This book is for readers of all levels of financial-savviness; I wouldn't expect you to read the first chapter on budgeting if you are far beyond that point. Similarly, if you're debt-free, don't bother with Section Four on Debt. Do I seem like the kind of person that wants to waste your time? Honey, no.

At the end of the book, I will also lay out an easy and clear-cut strategy that consists of 7 Simple Steps. The 7 Steps walk you through how to set up your savings accounts, from emergency and short-term savings to retirement. You'll also learn a painless strategy for paying off debt that you can implement right away. You'll know how many months it will take you to hit all of your financial goals so you can get your financial $hit together at last. You'll start to feel *good* about your money and have twice as much fun managing your finances going forward. Say goodbye to living paycheck-to-paycheck, because that will officially be a thing of the past. Say hello to transforming your life and not worrying about money anymore.

Countless millennials who struggle with their finances have already experienced an enormous sense of relief by implementing the tips and tricks I've included in this helpful guide. Most readers have several "Aha!" moments. You will too! By the end of this book, you will have a much better grasp of your situation and an enlightened sense of direction going forward.

Don't be the person who misses out on happy hour with friends because your account is overdrawn. Don't be the person who lives with the burden of $15,000 of credit card debt. Don't be the person who at age 70, *still* can't retire because of your lack of savings.

Instead, be the person that other people see and think, "She must make a ton of money." Not because you necessarily do, but because you manage your money like a boss and know what the hell you're doing. Be the kind of person that has your student loans paid off by age 25. Be the kind of person that takes action and does so immediately.

The money hacks you're about to read have been proven to create a path to 100% financial freedom. All you have to do to begin gaining control of your finances is keep reading. Each chapter will give you new insight that you can implement right away so you can get out of debt, save more, and have zero money probz. Take control of your situation right now by committing to read a chapter a day so that you can enjoy the prosperous life you've always desired.

Are you ready to think and act like the wealthy? Grab some popcorn and your Snuggie and keep reading. We're about to have some fun.

SECTION TWO: SAVINGS

Bada$$ Budgeting

TL;DR There is no hard and fast savings percentage rule because each situation is different. You must save a significant portion of your income. 10% won't get you anywhere. Up your savings game by increasing your income or decreasing your expenses.

Data from Gallup's 2013 Economy and Personal Finance survey found that two-thirds of American adults do not budget.[1] *Gasp!* How do people not track their spending? Household budgeting should be required by law – I'm dead serious. All financially successful people I know have a budget, so be like them. If you don't know how much extra money you have left over after your monthly expenses, how can you accomplish any financial goals?

"Wait a minute, Rachel! I don't have <u>any</u> extra money after expenses; I'm living paycheck to paycheck!" Calm down, missy! Plenty of people are in your situation. And while this book adds the most value to those who have extra money to save and invest, I will certainly help you get your expenses under control.

Although budgets are a dreaded activity, they're easier to create than you might think. A budget consists of a quick look at your income and expenses today as well as a goal for what you think your expenses should be. Easy-peasy.

Let's do a quick brainstorming session. Grab a beer, a pen, and a piece of paper, unless you're under 21 years old, in which case swap the beer for a Capri-Sun because those are equally delightful.

Seriously, go get some paper. Write down your after-tax monthly income at the top of the paper. Draw a smiley face next to it, because those are fun. Underneath, list all of your monthly expenses: both the category and amount per month. Don't forget to include your rent or mortgage, utilities, bills, insurance, transportation costs, food, entertainment, subscriptions, personal care, shopping, taxes, gifts and donations, credit card minimum payments, student loan minimum payments, and a little extra in case you forgot anything. If you don't know the exact amounts, it's okay to estimate them until you can find more accurate numbers.

Next, total up all of your expenses. Subtract your total monthly expenses from your total monthly income to calculate what you have leftover each month. Circle that number. That number is crucial. We shall call it your Golden Number, which represents your money left over after expenses. (Sidenote: Since I'm a kind and benevolent ruler, I've created worksheets that will do all of this for you, FO FREE! Go here to download: http://eepurl.com/c1ro7H)

Income : $2,740 ⌣

Expenses :
Rent $790
Utilities $120
Bills $65
Insurance $59
Car/gas $160
...   . ..
...   ...
...   ...

              $2,540

Golden Number : ($200)

The exercise you just completed will suffice for now. But, over the next month, I will require you to take it a step further and *track* these expenses. For example, what did you write down for you monthly food costs? Most people underestimate this category. The only way to know for sure is to track it for a month. I know; pain in the a$$, right? Luckily for us, there's an app for that: Mint. Download it, use it, worship it. Update your budget as you learn more about your spending habits. Here's an example of what a month of my spending has looked like in Mint in the past, when I was renting a room out from a friend to save money:

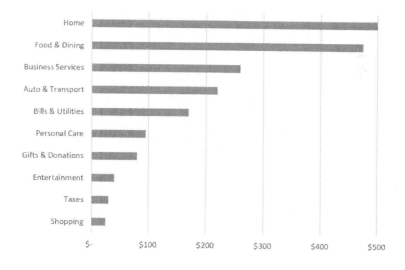

Remember to be thorough. Take gifts & donations as an example. Have you thought about what you spend on birthday gifts, bridal shower and wedding gifts, graduation gifts, and anniversary gifts, for every single friend and family member? Not to mention the biggies: Christmas, Hanukkah, and any other holiday you celebrate. Those expenses should all be included in the gifts & donations category.

As another example, let's consider subscriptions, which should include: magazines and newspapers, Netflix, Hulu, Amazon Prime, Costco, Apple Music, and anything else that you pay a recurring fee to use. Trust me when I say that you spend more in each category than you think.

Think about the little day-to-day stuff. If you go out for lunch and spend $10 every day during the work week, you're looking at $200 per month. If you get a manicure and pedicure every month, that's another $75 per month. It adds up fast!

As I said, you can write down estimates for now, but this is no quick exercise. It will take a month of true tracking—whether with pen and paper, or with an online app such as Mint—to understand what you're spending, so you can implement a budget.

Back to your Golden Number, which equals monthly income minus monthly expenses. *"What exact Golden Number should I aim for?"* you might ask. Yes, about that. You see, other money gurus advocate for "Save 10% of your paycheck!" "Save 15%!" "Save at least $500 per month!" Let me tell you why you should knowingly roll your eyes and chuckle in amusement when you hear a rule like that: Because there is NEVER one-size-fits-all when it comes to money management.

For a single woman making $500,000 per year with no plans to have kids and no debt, maybe saving 10%, which is $50,000 per year, will suffice for her goals. For the family of four bringing in $60,000 per year, that same 10%, which translates to $6,000 per year, won't get them far. In 30 years, they would have almost $200,000. So that will last them, what, three whole years in retirement? Slow. Clap.

Alas, you must begin somewhere, and I would suggest making sure your Golden Number is positive for starters. Then, focus on making your Golden Number larger. Your savings goal should be to save as much as humanly possible. Don't ever feel satisfied with saving 15%, or 20%, or 40%. For my whole life, I've found a way to save 50% of my income, regardless of whether I was making $30,000 or $60,000. I'll give you a goal: double your current Golden Number within the next six months. Get 'er done.

Help Me, I'm Poor

For those of you whose Golden Number needs beefing up (i.e. all of you), you must do one of two things, ASAP: increase your income or decrease your expenses. Easier said than done, right? I hate to be the bearer of bad news, but I won't be able to get you far if you are barely afloat as it is. $50 a month is not enough to fulfill your savings, investing, and retirement goals. Add another zero, and we might be getting somewhere.

I've got a nugget for you. Think about this: Your income potential is limitless. There is no cap on how much money you can make, since there are infinite opportunities to increase your income. However, there are limits on how much you can decrease your expenses. For example, your mortgage or rent payment is pretty non-negotiable. Because of these limitations, you can be more impactful if you work on increasing your income rather than focusing on decreasing your expenses. Or you can be a real winner and do BOTH. #MindBlown.

Increase Your Income

Here are some easy ways to increase your income. Some of these ideas will work for you, and some will be impossible for you, so take 'em or leave 'em:

- Ask for a raise or promotion (If you haven't received a raise in the last few years, do this—right meow)

- Work more: Longer hours or a second job

- Get a better-paying job

- Become a direct sales consultant or work at a multi-level marketing company

- Start a side hustle creating and selling products (Etsy, anyone?)

- Tutor local students

- Give music lessons (Probably only a good idea if you've played an instrument)

- Sell Cutco (my preferred method)

- Mow lawns and shovel snow

- Pet sit, house sit, babysit

- Walk people's dogs

- Sell your stuff: Poshmark, garage sale, Facebook groups

- Become an Uber or Lyft driver

- Rent out a spare room on AirBNB

- Flip furniture

- Donate plasma

- Do paid surveys online

I'm going to stop there because I think you get the picture. There are *tons* of ways to earn more income. Ever heard of Google? Good. Use it. I will recommend using Google multiple times throughout this book, and Google doesn't even pay me for that, sadly.

Decrease Your Expenses

Here are some ways to get your expenses to drop it like it's hot:

- Call your cable company and threaten to switch

- Call your cell phone company and threaten to switch

- Call your insurance company and threaten to switch

- Spend less money (my preferred method)

- Search for coupons and promo codes before you buy anything. Groceries, clothes, shampoo, backpacks, anything at all. You should never pay full price, period.

- Eat out less, cook more

- Live with your parents

- Get a roommate

- Get rid of your dog; pets are a huge expense (JOKING, PEOPLE)

- Carpool or use public transportation

- Lengthen the amount of time between highlights, manis, and pedis. Better yet, stop altogether.

- Unplug electrical devices when you're not using them

- Cancel club memberships and subscriptions

- Make your own coffee (the horror!)

Again, ideas are endless; please, Google for yourself.

At this point, you know what you're spending, and you've brainstormed ways to increase your income and decrease your expenses. Next: make a budget. As I said, a budget consists of a quick look at your income and expenses today as well as a goal for what you think your expenses should be. Once you've tracked your expenses for a month, you'll have a starting point to begin making adjustments. What are your highest spend categories? What have you been splurging on lately? What do you indulge in too often? What would be easiest to cut back on? Challenge yourself to find a way to save in each and every category, even if it's only a few dollars.

Consider how effortlessly money slips through your fingers on the little stuff. The coffee concept is overused but worth stating: Spending $5 a day on your fancy coffee amounts to almost $2,000 per year. Want a $2,000 raise? Congratulations, I just gave you one. That $30 per month gym membership you never go to? Cancel it and save yourself $360 for the year. Going out for appetizers and drinks for $30 after work might not sound like a lot, but when you do that twice a week, it's costing you over $3,000 per year. Get the picture?

You can also work backwards. What do you want your monthly expenses to be? Decide on that number and decrease every category until you get there. Be realistic, but eliminate, eliminate, eliminate. You can always add items back in later.

Creating a budget is easy. Sticking to it? Not so much. You'll need to commit to this—for yourself and for your future. This exercise should not be taken lightly. Be sure to track your expenses for a month before you put time into creating a new budget. Then, stick to your new plan!

Hacks are a girl's best friend. I already talked about the amazing app and website called Mint; now allow me to introduce you to Honey, Acorn, and Qapital. Honey is a free service that makes it ridiculously easy to save time and money online. It's a browser extension that searches and detects coupons and applies them at checkout. #Genius. Go to JoinHoney.com to download your next best friend. Acorn is a cool service that invests your spare change for $1/month. You link your credit and debit cards, and then when you buy a $5.39 Starbucks latte, Acorn rounds the purchase up to $6.00 and invests that extra 61 cents for you. Super easy to "magically" save a couple hundo with Acorn. Lastly, Qapital is a nifty and free service that automates your savings according to goals and rules that you set.

#ToughLove

"Ugh, this sounds too hard already. Isn't there another way?" No. You don't get to say this. I'm going to be tough on you for a sec. Depriving yourself of your daily Starbucks Frappuccino isn't hard. Moving back in with your parents isn't hard. Getting a second job isn't hard. Wanna know what's freaking hard? *Cancer* is hard. *Getting deployed* is hard. *Losing a loved one* is hard. Got it? You don't get to say that getting your finances in order is "too hard." It's a

practical thing that all successful adults do. Get with the program.

Nobody ever said this was a cakewalk. If you are barely making enough to cover your expenses, you *must change your circumstances.* Adapting to something new is always challenging, but you need to put your big girl pants on and deal with it. Why? Because stressing about how you're going to survive until your next paycheck is no way to live your life. You. Must. Be. Better.

And as I said before, there are only two ways to be better. Make more money or spend less. Ever want to get ahead in life? Good. Make it happen. I promise you will feel great once you do. If you ever get down on yourself, remember: you smell like pine needles, and you have a face like sunshine.

So again: get your income up and your expenses down. Need a more concrete plan of action? Good news: entire books have been written on this one tiny subject. A few I'd recommend as a starting point are:

1. "Total Money Makeover," by Dave Ramsey, for getting out of debt

2. "I Will Teach You to Be Rich," by Ramit Sethi, for simple money-saving tricks

3. "Rich Dad, Poor Dad," by Robert Kiyosaki, for wealth-building tools

For most people, gaining control of their finances is a matter of getting out of debt or living a simpler life style. Each situation is unique, so there isn't a single solution for everyone. Until you can increase your income or lower your expenses, you won't be able to incorporate a lot of the strategy I have outlined in this book. Get started right now by listing out ten specific ways you can make more and ten specific ways you can spend less. Circle your favorite two in each category and get on it.

Savings: Anotha Day Anotha Dolla

TL;DR Open a high-yield savings account to take advantage of compound interest and grow your money. Separate your savings into four buckets depending on how soon you will need the money. Bucket #1 is for emergencies, Bucket #2 is for big-ticket items within the next year, Bucket #3 is for big-ticket items more than a year away, and Bucket #4 is for retirement. Fill up Bucket #1 first, then work on Bucket #2 and #3 while contributing regularly to Bucket #4.

Americans suck at saving money, it turns out. 19% of Americans have NOTHING set aside to cover an emergency.[2] Uh, no wonder everyone is in debt! ValuePenguin reports that if you are under 35 years old, you only have $1,580 saved on average![3] Did your jaw just drop? It should have! Oh, and also, one-third of Americans have *zero* saved for retirement.[4] SMH.

Ladies and gents, you have two financial goals. They are:

1. Increase your assets

2. Reduce your liabilities

That's all you need to know. Do I even need to write the rest of this book? Fine, I'll keep going.

So that we are all on the same page, allow me to define assets and liabilities for you. Assets are items that *add* to your net worth: cash, savings accounts, 401(K)s, the value of your house, money that someone else owes you, and so forth. Liabilities are items that *subtract* from your net worth: loans, credit card debt, the mortgage on your house, money that you owe someone else, and so forth. Here's how it all works together:

Assets - Liabilities = Net Worth

Therefore, to grow your net worth, you must *increase* your assets and/or *decrease* your liabilities.

I urge you to track your net worth via a balance sheet each month. This exercise can be eye-opening and FUN! (I'm serious!) Here's an example of a balance sheet:

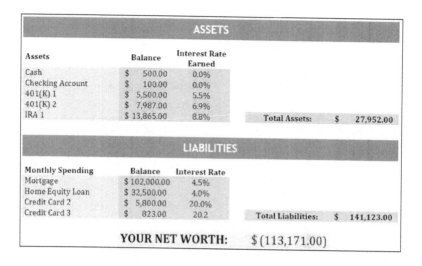

ASSETS					
Assets	Balance	Interest Rate Earned			
Cash	$ 500.00	0.0%			
Checking Account	$ 100.00	0.0%			
401(K) 1	$ 5,500.00	5.5%			
401(K) 2	$ 7,987.00	6.9%			
IRA 1	$ 13,865.00	8.8%	Total Assets:	$	27,952.00
LIABILITIES					
Monthly Spending	Balance	Interest Rate			
Mortgage	$ 102,000.00	4.5%			
Home Equity Loan	$ 32,500.00	4.0%			
Credit Card 2	$ 5,800.00	20.0%			
Credit Card 3	$ 823.00	20.2	Total Liabilities:	$	141,123.00
YOUR NET WORTH:			$ (113,171.00)		

You can download this exact balance sheet for free at http://eepurl.com/c1ro7H, courtesy of yours truly.

Earning Interest

Magic exists. It exists in the form of continuously compounded interest. This beautiful mathematical concept explains how you can put $10,000 in savings today, do nothing for 30 years, and then – BAM – have $44,816.89 (assuming 5% continuously compounded interest.) I'm not making this $hit up. Fill up your wine glass and take a seat so I can explain this to you.

#DeetsPlz

You earn interest by putting your money in a savings vehicle that offers to pay you interest. It's like a bank saying, "Pick me, choose me, love me; I'll even pay you!" The money paid is calculated based on the interest rate they're offering.

Allow me to break down the term continuously compounded interest, starting with compounded. Compounded means that the interest you are earning is added to the principal amount of a deposit. In other words, you are earning interest on your interest.

Let's throwback to Algebra II for a second. You deposit $100 in your savings account, which earns 10% interest per year or $10. So after one year, you have $110. What happens in year two? In year two, you get 10% interest again, but this time it's based on the $110 amount, so you earn $11. After year 2, you have $121. See how that works? Your interest is added to the total amount so that every year, you will earn more and more dollars in interest! This is why Albert Einstein is said to have called compound interest the greatest mathematical discovery of all time.

#MathingOver. What does *continuously* compounded mean? Interest can be compounded in any time period. In the example above, interest was compounded annually. It can also be compounded semi-annually, monthly, daily, or even continuously. The more frequently the interest is compounded, the more you will earn overall. I could bore you with the details and formulas, but how about not. Just know that a bank account offering 1% interest compounded daily is more attractive than a bank account offering 1% interest compounded annually. Below are a few banks I would recommend for savings based on personal use, but you can also do a quick Google search of "best high yield online savings accounts."

- Ally Online Savings
- Barclays Online Savings (what I currently use)
- Alliant Credit Union
- GS Bank

A quick word on Annual Percentage Yield (APY.) APY is a standardized representation of an interest rate, based on a compounding period of one year. Let's say you're trying to compare several interest rates from several banks. However these interest rates are compounded, whether monthly or daily or continuously, the APY converts them into a per year rate so you can compare them evenly. Higher is better. Bottom line: when you are comparing interest rates offered by different banks, you always want to compare the APY since it accounts for differing compounding schedules.

Understanding how interest works (and why it's so important) is vital to setting up your various savings accounts so you can achieve your goals. Also, knowing that there are banks offering over 1% APY versus your checking account which offers 0.01% APY will help you put your money to work. #KnowledgeIsPower. Next, let's take a look at your savings strategy.

Savings Buckets

Let's talk about growing your assets; specifically, your cash or checking accounts, savings accounts, investment accounts, and retirement accounts.

Your cash on hand or checking account will always be fluid, which means immediately available to spend. If you have just received a paycheck, you might have lots of available cash. Or, if you are a college student, you might have $3.81 to your name in which case, I raise my glass to you in remembrance of times gone by.

Savings is a whole different ball game. That's because sometimes you are saving for an urgent car repair, sometimes you are saving for your wedding that's a year away, sometimes you are saving for retirement when you turn 60, and sometimes you are saving so you can go get a few martinis after work (been there, girlfriend.) Since we all have different, and often multiple, savings goals, please humor me and envision four buckets. Bucket #1 is Emergency Savings. Bucket #2 is Medium-Term Savings: one year or less. Bucket #3 is Long-Term Savings: greater than one year but before retirement. Bucket #4 is Retirement Savings.

Remember your Golden Number? That's what you'll use to fill up the four buckets. Bucket #1 for Emergency Savings should hold at least $1,000. This will cover any unknown expenses that come up suddenly, such as the heating system in your house malfunctioning in the middle of winter. Bucket #1 covers expenses for which you were not prepared but that must be remedied right away, AKA *Unforeseeable And Urgent Expenses*. These funds should always be easily accessible, meaning you should be able to withdraw them instantaneously. You can keep this money in your checking account, in a savings account that you can access immediately, or even in your sock drawer. Don't worry about what interest rate you earn; this money's only job is to be available when needed. Also, friendly reminder: those amazing heels that you saw at the mall are *not* an emergency, sadly.

Bucket #2 for Medium-Term Savings is first and foremost a secondary emergency bucket. It must contain enough money to hold you over for three to six months should you lose your job. Calculate how much money it takes you to survive for one month, multiply that by 4.5, and make sure you have *at least* that amount in Bucket #2. I hope you don't have to thank me later. Bucket #2 is also used for whatever you are saving for within the next 12 months. This might include buying a car, going on a vacation, completing a house project, or buying an engagement ring. You don't need both components: you need whichever is greater. If your 4.5 months' worth of expenses is $30,000, and you are saving for $20,000 worth of stuff within the next 12 months, then Bucket #2 should hold $30,000.

Since Bucket #2 will be accessed within the year, I would recommend keeping this in a high-yield savings account rather than investing this money in the stock market. If you invest money in the stock market and pull it out in less than a year, you have to pay this unfortunate thing called short-term capital gains taxes. To avoid this tax, I recommend only investing money in the stock market that can stay there for more than a year. So put Bucket #2 in a high-yield savings account where you can withdraw money in a few business days if needed, but where you will still earn more interest than in a checking account.

Bucket #3 for Long-Term Savings will hold whatever you are saving for that is more than a year away but prior to retirement. If you're 12 years of age, you'll want to use this bucket to start saving for your wedding since those cost $40,000 these days. #WishIWasKidding. In all seriousness, future weddings and honeymoons would fall in Bucket #3 for most people. Saving up money to buy a house is another great example for this bucket. I recommend investing Bucket #3 in the stock market, where it will likely grow a lot more than in a savings account.

Finally, you have Bucket #4 for retirement savings. If you're around my age, this is pretty far off, and you won't need to access this money for several decades. This money should be kept in an IRA, 401(K), or other retirement account. Please, do yourself a favor and envision your retirement account like a jail cell for your cash. You *cannot* access this money until you retire. Okay, okay, I won't lie to you: In reality, you can access this money whenever you want, but depending on the type of account, you normally will be required to pay taxes and a hefty penalty fee if you withdraw it before you reach retirement age. So, for our purposes, do not contribute to Bucket #4 unless you know without a doubt that you will not need that money until you retire. Because trust me, if you *do* have to withdraw money early, it *hurts*. Since Bucket #4 will ultimately require a lot more cash than the other buckets, you'll be contributing to this regularly for the rest of your life. Welcome to Adulting.

If you can't already tell, the four buckets are divided based on ease of accessing the money, which is called *liquidity*. These buckets exist because sometimes you need to access your money right away for emergencies, but sometimes you won't touch it for 40 years and therefore can lock it up in a retirement account. You may feel that $1,000 is not enough for emergency savings, or that Bucket #3 doesn't apply to you because you have no savings goals that fit in that category, or that you'd rather not invest your long-term savings in the stock market at all, and that's your prerogative. But this structure will work wonders for you, and you can customize it based on your own needs.

I will be strict on this: you must <u>fill up Bucket #1 first!</u> You need some sort of emergency savings before you start saving for anything else. This ensures that *when*, not if, you have an emergency, you will be adequately prepared.

Let me stop you right here. This is an opportune moment for some more brainstorming so you can set this system up for yourself. Get your cherry-spiced rum, pen, and paper. Go on, I'll wait.

On your paper draw four big buckets and number them 1 through 4. Obviously, when I'm talking about buckets, I'm envisioning champagne buckets.

For Bucket #1, write $1,000.

Next: remember the monthly expenses that you estimated earlier? Multiply your total monthly expenses by 4.5 and write down that number in Bucket #2. The reason for this calculation is that you need to have three to six months' worth of living expenses in Bucket #2 in case your a$$ gets fired. Bucket #2 ensures you have enough to live off of if you are ever out of a job for an extended period of time.

Now, for Buckets #2 and #3, brainstorm all the items or experiences you want to save for within the next year (write those for Bucket #2) and that are more than a year away (Bucket #3.) Here's a list to jog your memory: buy a house, buy a car, buy a boat, go on a trip, plan a wedding, buy an engagement ring, complete a house project or renovation, enroll in college, have a baby, and so forth. Once you have finished brainstorming, jot down dollar estimates next to each item and add them all up.

Pause. Look at what you brainstormed for things you want to save for within the next year in Bucket #2: Is the total amount greater than your 4.5 months' worth of expenses figure? If so, circle the former number. Or is your one-year savings goal number less than your 4.5 months' worth of expenses figure? Circle the salary figure instead.

Now you should have a total dollar amount for Bucket #2 and #3. So far, your paper should look something like this:

(Jealous of my pretty picture? Download the excel version for free at http://eepurl.com/c1ro7H.)

Yeah, yeah, we didn't do Bucket #4. I hate to break it to ya, but if your retirement is more than 20 years out, neither you nor I have any idea how much money you will need for retirement. You can estimate it, yes, but there are so many unknown variables between now and then that even the best estimate is nothing but a guess. The exception is if you are nearing retirement, which in that case, put your best estimate down.

I could write an entire book about retirement (sequel?), but I won't; so I will let you research all that goodness for yourself. I could also give you a goal (save 15% of each paycheck!), but that is meaningless without knowing your particular circumstances. The bottom line is, retiring requires a LOT of money—we're talking six zeroes—so you need to save as much as you can. You can put a big ole question mark for now in Bucket #4. We will discuss your retirement plan in more detail later on.

Let's talk strategy. How do you fill up these buckets? I will prioritize for you. Bucket #1 is first. Even if you have to stop contributing to your retirement account for a couple months so you can fill up Bucket #1, DO SO. There is nothing more important than having at least $1,000 in emergency savings tucked away. If you don't have an emergency fund, you'll be thrown off your savings game later on when an emergency happens, which will discourage you. Once you check that off, we can talk about how to distribute your money between Buckets #2, #3, and #4.

Bucket #1 is the most important. Next most important? Bucket #4. Yes, retirement is far off, and you want to save for the things you know you'll need within the next year, but if you do not start saving for retirement right now, you won't ever retire. Let me repeat that since you've had a couple alcoholic beverages: if you do not start saving for retirement *right now*, you won't ever retire.

So once Bucket #1 is full and happy (like you are right now), you will contribute regularly to Bucket #4. I would personally contribute as much as possible while also hitting my most important savings goals for Buckets #2 and #3, but even $50 per month is better than nothing! And you could always follow the 10% to 15% per paycheck rule, but like I said earlier, that's pretty meaningless since you don't know how much you'll need for retirement. More on this to come.

After Buckets #1 and #4, Bucket #2 is next in priority because it is where you'll pull money from if you ever lose your job. This bucket should hold at least three to six months of living expenses or whatever savings goals you've outlined for the next year, whichever is larger. So after filling up Bucket #1, and contributing regularly to Bucket #4, I would put the rest of your Golden Number in Bucket #2 until that's full. Then, naturally, once Bucket #2 is full, fill up Bucket #3. Ya dig?

You might be frustrated with me since this seems so abstract. This exercise will differ for every individual. There is no hard and fast rule. Put your big girl panties on and use your brain to determine what makes the most sense for you and your circumstances. If you've made it this far and you understand that you'll eventually fill up your first three buckets while contributing to Bucket #4 regularly, you're in great shape.

"*Wait a second Rachel! My Golden Number is barely big enough to split between all these buckets!*" Yes, there are a lot of buckets. But you can never have too many buckets. Also, I never said that this would happen overnight. It could take several paychecks to fill up Bucket #1. Depending on your savings goals, it could even take an entire year to fill up Bucket #1 and Bucket #2. That's okay! Progress is progress, and as long as you do it in the order I've outlined, you'll be dandy. I would not expect you to have $50,000 in savings overnight.

Hopefully you can now see why your Golden Number is so important, and why you should increase your income and decrease your expenses. Growing your Golden Number means hitting your savings goals faster, which means growing your assets and therefore your net worth. Do your best, educate yourself, and believe in yourself.

SECTION THREE: DEBT

There is No Good Debt. Only Tolerable Debt.

TL;DR There's no such thing as good debt; it's either tolerable debt or bad debt. Compare your financing rate to the underlying asset's rate of appreciation to know for sure if you are making the right choice before going into debt.

Just for $hits and giggles, please indulge me by going to the website www.USDebtClock.org. I'm looking at it right now and fighting off a minor panic attack.

Americans hold over $999 billion in credit card debt.[5] That number is followed by NINE zeroes: $999,000,000,000. Of credit card debt. Hold my drink while I attempt to remain calm.

Further, the average American student loan debt is $50,000, and the average household is $163,000 in debt.[6] WHYYY?

What are your two financial goals again?

1. Increase your assets—by growing your golden number so you can allocate more between your four buckets.

2. Reduce your liabilities—by paying down debt.

For starters, what is debt? Debt is a liability, an IOU, an amount owed to someone else. Examples include your home mortgage, car loan, student loans, credit card debt, or any other financial amount that is owed or due. Borrow $100 from your friend? You're in debt to her.

Believe it or not, there is no such thing as "good" debt. What most people would view as good debt, I view as tolerable debt. On the other end of the spectrum is bad debt. Pay attention girlfriend, because I don't want you mixing these up!

Tolerable debt vs. bad debt

My definition of tolerable debt is, generally, debt that backs an appreciating asset. Appreciating = increasing in value. Picture your house, which is one of the only examples of tolerable debt. You have the value of your house, which is an asset, and then you have your mortgage, which is a liability or debt. More often than not, one would expect her house to appreciate in value. Going into debt to acquire an asset that will appreciate in value usually makes sense.

Going into debt to acquire that Coach purse does not. Get the picture?

By this definition, we can classify your car loan and credit card debt as bad debt. Car values don't go anywhere but down, and whatever you purchased on your credit card likely has zero resale value the moment you buy it.

Time for a quiz! This scenario is inspired by a real story. Ross and Emily (names have been changed) use their home equity line of credit to purchase a painting on their honeymoon for $3,000. Ten years later, the painting is worth $10,000. Tolerable debt or bad debt? Tolerable, because the painting's value increased.

Now for a caveat: what if Ross and Emily put this painting on their credit card, on which they pay 20% interest, and the painting was only worth $4,000 after ten years? By my definition, the asset appreciated, so it's tolerable debt, right? WRONG. Please note that my definition above is *in general*. There are always exceptions to the rule, and to know if something is truly tolerable debt or bad debt requires some rate comparisons. What we want to do is compare the rate at which they are borrowing money to the rate at which the asset's value increases. In other words, are you paying 25% in interest to only realize 10% in appreciation on whatever you bought? Because if so, that makes zero sense. Zero... cents. HA!

In the example above, Ross and Emily are paying 20% in interest per year. In the span of ten years, the painting's value increases from $3,000 to $4,000. Therefore, the painting's value is increasing at a rate of about 3% per year. How did I figure that out? I Googled, "compound interest calculator." No need to turn this into rocket science.

So would you pay 20% in interest for a 3% return? I think not. Therefore, in this example, buying the painting is bad debt.

Let's do one more example, or if you're like, "Rachel, I got this," then skip ahead.

Let's say your boyfriend buys an engagement ring that costs $1,000. Boyfriend Charming takes advantage of the jewelry store's 1% financing for three years. After three years, the ring is worth $2,000. So, what is your gut reaction? Was this "investment" worth it?

Googles

Hell yeah that's worth it! That sucker is appreciating in value at a rate of over 20% per year compared to the store's 1% financing!

Friends, let's be real. When you buy something like an engagement ring or painting, you know nothing about whether it will appreciate in value. You may speculate, but you won't know until you know. I would recommend *not* purchasing any asset in the hopes or expectation that it will appreciate. I'm not an art expert or a diamond professional, and I would never go into debt to buy either one of these things. In reality, there are few examples of tolerable debt, and there's not much for which I'd be willing to go into debt. Why take that risk? Even your house, as the crash of 2008 proved, will not always increase in value. Do your homework before going into debt for *any* investment. Long story short, almost all debt is bad debt.

Debt: An Emotional Burden

Think about debt in itself. If you have *any* debt, you are not financially free. You owe money to someone. That's a burden, a weight you carry with you. Maybe you think I'm being dramatic, but can you imagine how good it would feel to owe nothing to anyone else? To not have to make payments? To be financially independent? For that psychological relief, I personally would go to great lengths to avoid being in debt, and you should be thinking like that too. Rid yourself of it, whenever possible.

"But, but!" Yeah, yeah, I know what you're going to say. What about student loans? That has to be tolerable debt, right? Patience, young grasshopper. Coming right up.

In the following chapters, you'll learn the importance of building a good credit score and where you can find your own credit report for free. I will also teach you about the various types of debt: student loans, credit card debt, home mortgages, and home equity loans, to name a few.

Credit Score: A GPA For Your Finances

TL;DR You need good credit to buy big-ticket items and to qualify for lower insurance rates. The three main credit reporting agencies are TransUnion, Equifax, and Experian. The main factors that influence your credit score are payment history, debt utilization, length of credit history, number of inquiries, and number and type of credit accounts.

Do you ever see yourself purchasing a mansion or Lamborghini, or even opening your own business? Say hi to a little something called a credit score. Or, Option B: pay for everything in cash. I am currently in love with Option B.

However, it's been heartbreak from the get-go, because Option B is out of my reach. It's out of your reach too unless you have a cool $150,000 lying around for whenever you decide to buy that Lambo. Sigh.

Assuming Option B will remain #goalz for now, let's focus on the first option: building credit.

You want to have good credit for several reasons. Your credit score is the figure many businesses use to determine if you're reliable or trustworthy. For example:

1. A good credit rating lowers your homeowners, auto, and life insurance rates. Lower rates free up your cash for better, funner things. Win.

2. A good credit rating helps you gain employment, because many employers run credit checks on potential employees. Don't be the person that gets a red flag on this portion of a job application.

3. Credit often offers protection against fraud and identity theft. That's because most credit cards will reimburse you for any fraudulent spends, and many alert you if they notice suspicious activity on your account.

4. A good credit rating helps you with renting, which you'll need to do until you can buy a home.

Long story short: credit is vital. And you need to start building it, like, yesterday.

I hate to say this, but the best way to build credit is by opening a credit card. The reason I hate to say this is because it's difficult for many people to "control" their spending when they have access to credit. Please read Chapter Seven on credit cards carefully, so that you are up close and personal with all the scary things that go along with them.

If you have no credit history, your best bet is to apply for a credit card with a low credit limit. There are tons of student-friendly credit cards these days. My first ever CC was the Discover It card and my first ever credit limit was $1,500. If you have trouble qualifying for a credit card because of your lack of credit history, you may need to get a co-signer. This means having a family member or friend vouch for you by backing the loan with their good name and credit rating. A third option to begin building credit is becoming an authorized user on someone else's credit card.

Use the credit card like you would a debit card. Pay it in full every single month. Pay. It. In. Full. Every. Single. Month. Incorporate the card for routine purchases, pay off your bill in full like clockwork, and voilá. You're building credit.

Make 100% of your payments on time, not only with your credit cards, but also utilities, other bills, rent, and so forth. Bills that go unpaid could be sent to a collection agency, which would ruin your credit. So, keep it 100, and never miss a payment on anything. You can even ensure that you won't miss a payment by setting up automatic, full payments; all credit cards allow you to do this.

Credit Reporting

There are three major credit reporting agencies: Equifax, TransUnion, and Experian. Until you have a credit card, student loan, or some other type of credit, these agencies won't have the deets on you. What do these agencies do? They compile details about your credit history into a report so that potential lenders can see the type of risk they'd be taking in giving you a new credit card or loan. Most of the information they compile can remain on your credit reports indefinitely; that's why you have to be A+ with it. FYI: The three companies operate independently, so your credit score could vary from one to the next.

Federal law entitles you to one free credit report from each bureau every twelve months, so, three per year. However, most consumers have constant access to their credit score. Many credit card companies offer free credit reporting as a perk. The website CreditKarma is free; I check my scores there a couple times per week.

It's important to check your credit more often than three times per year. That's because of this fun little thing called identity theft that can throw your life into shambles. I'm talking worse than liking your ex's pic on Instagram from 23 weeks ago. Basically, if people get a hold of your name, SSN, and birthdate, then they can pretend to be you and apply for credit cards and loans, spend the money, and then if YOU don't pay, it hurts your score. These criminals are difficult to catch. That's why I monitor my score weekly. It's a preventative measure, like getting your teeth cleaned. Protect yourself and check your credit on the reg.

Credit Score Factors

Credit scores range from 300 to 850, and the higher your score is, the better. Most lenders won't approve an application for a mortgage loan if your credit is under 600, to give you an idea. Your goal is to get your credit score as close to 850 as possible. For reference, the average FICO score in America is 695,[7] but since readers of *Money Honey* are extra let's aim for 750 at least.

Here's what will impact your score:

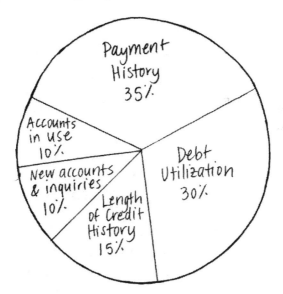

1. Payment History. Whether you pay on time or not accounts for about 35% of your score, so even one late payment can have a ginormous negative impact. Pay in full, on time, every time. Another part of your

credit history is public records, which would include things like bankruptcies, judgments, and collection items.

2. Debt Utilization. This is how much of your total credit line you are using, and the lower, the better. For example, someone using all $5,000 of her $5,000 credit line looks slightly credit-crazy compared with someone only using a couple hundred bucks. You can maintain a healthy utilization by paying off your balance every month. Debt utilization accounts for about 30% of your score. Easy trick: request credit line increases every year or so on your credit cards. When your credit line increases and you continue to spend the same low amount, your debt utilization decreases, which helps your credit score.

3. Length of Credit History. If you're young or starting to build your credit, you're unfortunately at a disadvantage. Lenders like to see older accounts established a long time ago. This accounts for about 15% of your score, which is why closing your oldest credit account is typically ill-advised.

4. New accounts and inquiries. Opening multiple new accounts in a short period of time may look shady to potential lenders. Also, whenever someone else pulls your credit report, such as a lender, landlord, or insurer, an inquiry is recorded on your credit report. The fewer inquiries, the better. This accounts for about 10% of your score.

5. Accounts in use. Consumers with a higher number of credit accounts generally have better scores, especially if they have a mix of different types of credit. This accounts for about 10% of your score.

The bottom line is to always pay on time, only use a small amount of your overall credit, keep your oldest accounts open to increase your average length of credit history, don't have too many credit inquiries, and make sure you have a healthy mix of different types of credit. Doing these five things will get you as close to 850 as possible.

Student Debt—Fannie Mae, Mae, Go Away

TL;DR Considering going to college? The cost of college these days is a significant financial burden and may not be financially viable. Recently graduated? Student loan payments can be consolidated at a lower interest rate to save you money. Saving for your child's education? Parents can take advantage of the tax benefits of a 529 plan.

The student loan industry is insane. Millennials don't expect to pay off their student loans until they are 35, and

23% of millennial workers are delaying having children because of outstanding student loans.[8] Get smart and don't let student loans rule your life!

Pre-College: Is it worth it?

There's such a strong perception in the United States that you must have a college degree to be successful. I won't take that debate on, but with the cost of getting a degree soaring to an all-time high, it's worth our time to inspect this investment a little further. So let's go there: Is it worth it to go into tens of thousands of dollars of debt to get a college degree? I hate to be the bearer of bad news, but it is, quite literally, impossible to predict the value of your college degree.

Here's where some of you will throw statistics at me: "The average engineer makes $70,000 right out of college!" "Most nurses make a starting salary of $50,000!" So, you claim that you can, quite literally, calculate whether your student loans are worth it.

Bless your heart. Averages are all well and good, but how do you know with 100% certainty what YOU will be making straight out of college? Unless you're a psychic—and if you are, please write to me immediately—you don't know. At all.

Don't get me wrong; this approach of assessing the value of a college degree and what you might earn in your chosen career is worthwhile. I support the notion of completing a cost/benefit analysis, but I caution you against taking the numbers too literally.

I have a financial economics degree. When I graduated in 2013, the average straight-outta-college worker with my degree was making around $60,000. Guess how much I started off making? $36,000. And this is coming from a 3.99 GPA student, ranked #3 in her class, who graduated in three years. Huge wake-up call. Yuge. (Don't feel too bad for me! I'm making more now.)

For those of you who argue that you can precisely calculate the rate of return on your college degree, using the total cost of your education and the net present value of your future earnings, please don't. The unknown here is your future earnings. You won't know how much your college degree is worth until you get out in the workforce and start making money, and by then, it's not like you can go back and undo it if it turned out to be a sucky investment. You might have an idea, but you don't know.

Another thought to consider is opportunity cost: the lost opportunity of taking those same four years and getting a low-paying job instead of funding a college degree. Or taking that same $30,000 of student loan money and starting a business instead. You should consider all avenues of how that money and time could have been spent.

Referring back to the previous chapter, going into debt in the expectation that a certain asset will appreciate in value, or be worth a certain amount, is pure stupidity. The college degree debate is tough. What opportunities exist these days for someone with no college degree in a country where having a college degree is like owning a pair of pants? On the other hand, how do you know what an acceptable amount of student loan debt is if you don't know how much you'll be making? I'm not going to pretend to have a tidy answer for every financial question when more often than not there *is* no answer. Taking on student debt is entirely circumstantial and, in the end, you need to do what's right for you. But please don't be one of those people who borrow $60,000 for a Fine Arts degree. Do your research and at least try to make your way into a growing, high-paying industry, while working to earn as many scholarships as possible. That's your best bet.

Pursue your passions on the *side*. If you can make a living pursuing your passion, then by all means, don't let me stop you. But if you can't, then you must make a living first, and only then pursue your passions. You heard me: Don't follow your dreams if they can't make you any money! That might be the most controversial thing I write in this book (next to, "you're an idiot if you think having a $40,000 wedding is unavoidable"), and I'm okay with that.

Post-College: Paying your student loans

I have one word to describe receiving your first student loan bill: poop. And like poop, student loan payments are unavoidable.

Most questions I receive about student loans are centered around debt consolidation. Graduating from school and paying three separate amounts to three loan servicers is common. To avoid this, you can "consolidate" your debt, which means combining all your loans into one principal.

There are two types of student loan consolidation: federal and private. Federal consolidation is done through the Department of Education, and it will not lower your interest rate or save you money. In fact, it may even *increase* your interest rate, or lengthen the repayment term, which means you'll end up paying more in interest throughout the life of your loan. If you go this route, do your research.

The benefits of federal student loan consolidation are twofold: 1) Sometimes you must go through this process to become eligible for some federal loan repayment programs, and 2) it makes things simpler. Consolidation, in either case, results in a single monthly payment instead of multiple payments at different times to different loan servicers.

Private student loan consolidation, on the other hand, is done through a private lender, and the primary benefit is that you could qualify for a lower interest rate, thereby saving you money. To me, the obvious choice is private consolidation. Why even bother if you can't save money overall?

Here are some questions to ask yourself if you're considering consolidating your student loans:

- What is my main goal? For example, if you want to save money by getting a lower interest rate, go with private consolidation. If you're struggling to make ends meet and need a smaller monthly payment, opt for a consolidation that will let you extend your repayment term and therefore lower your monthly payments.

- How much can I afford to pay each month?

- What is my credit score? Better credit scores = better interest rates.

- Can I combine both federal and private student loans? Short answer: usually no.

Keep in mind that you can do an income-based repayment plan for your federal loans, so you might want to consider taking advantage of that before consolidating.

If you're considering student loan consolidation, some companies to check out are SoFi, Earnest, DRB, and Citizens Bank.

Should I pay more than the minimum amount?

Like most things, what you should pay depends on the circumstances: how much you already have saved in your Buckets, how much you should be saving, what your expenses are, what your income is, and what other debt you have. That's a lot of variables to consider. I, however, will always advocate that you pay off your debt as quickly as possible.

Let's take my bada$$ sister Lauren, who graduated with over $20,000 in debt. Lauren began working as a postpartum nurse after graduating. She moved back in with our parents to save money and keep her expenses to a minimum. She used an old "junk" car to get around. She didn't have any credit card debt because she's a smarty-pants. Her only liability was her student debt and she decided to take it head on. She had all this extra money and instead of spending it on trips or shoes or meaningless CRAP, she put it all towards her student loan payments. She paid off almost half of it in ONE YEAR! Someone in her situation should *absolutely* be paying more than the minimum payment because *why the heck wouldn't you?* Bottom line: Be cool. Be like Lauren.

Not everyone is that fortunate. Most people are juggling multiple kinds of debt and don't have a ton of extra money to spare. In that scenario, knowing whether you should be paying more than your minimum payment is a little trickier. Later on, I'll go through a detailed strategy on how to balance all your debt and savings goals, because it can be overwhelming to decide where to put your money when your money is limited.

Parenthood: Saving For Your Child's College Education

The cost of attending college is YIKES. Four years at a private non-profit college, including tuition, fees, and room and board, costs roughly $175,000, and a public four-year in-state college, while less expensive, costs close to $80,000.[9] Many young people are turning to student loans to fund the cost of college education, placing a strain on their finances beyond graduation.

Moms and Dads, if you're worried about the financial burden this will place on your child, allow me to introduce you to the 529 Plan. A 529 Plan is a tax-advantaged savings plan sponsored by a state or state agency, designed to encourage saving for future education costs. Each state has its own 529 plan, but generally, each plan can be used to meet costs of qualified colleges in another state. Therefore, you're not limiting the beneficiary to attending college in a certain area. Below is a quick walkthrough of the benefits and disadvantages of a 529 plan.

Benefits:

1. Tax breaks! Contributions are not deductible, but earnings in a 529 plan grow federal-tax-free and won't be taxed when the money is taken out to pay for college. Many states also offer tax breaks.

2. The donor (you) stays in control of the account. Thus, the named beneficiary—your child—has no legal rights to the funds, so you can assure the money will be used for its intended purpose.

3. Low maintenance. All contributions can be set up to automatically invest in whatever you pick.

4. Flexibility. Anyone can open a 529 plan. Unlike retirement accounts, there are no income limits, age limits, or annual contribution limits. Also, anyone

can contribute to a 529 plan that you open, meaning that grandparents, other relatives, or non-relatives can gift to an existing account. Further, 529 assets can be used at any eligible institution of higher education. That includes not only four-year colleges, but also qualifying two-year associate degree programs, trade schools, and vocational schools.

Drawbacks:

The obvious question is, what if your child reaches the age of 18 and decides NOT to go to college? What happens to all the money you've contributed to the 529 plan? The easiest route is to change the designated beneficiary to another member of the family. There are no tax consequences or penalties to do this. So, if you have another child, this is your best bet. You could also save the funds for a future grandchild. Heck, you can even change the beneficiary to yourself and pursue that grad degree.

However, if you have no one else to spend this money on for educational purposes, prepare to be subjected not only to taxes but also a ten percent federal penalty on the earnings portion of the withdrawal. Your contributions were made with after-tax money and therefore will not be taxed or penalized, but all the earnings will be. This would be the same scenario if you overfunded the account and your child didn't use it all or received more scholarships than expected. This is the main reason that I'm not a huge fan of 529 plans. For many families and circumstances, they are amazing. But you can't predict the future, and if your child doesn't end up going to college, you wasted a huge tax benefit that could've been put towards your own retirement. And that would seriously suck.

A 529 plan may not be suitable for those working with short time horizons. If college is only a year or a few years away, then the benefit of tax-free growth is limited. It may not be worth the hassle. These plans are most beneficial when they are started years in advance, and the money is given time to grow. The key is to start early. Like, when you are in labor.

Credit Cards—Friend or Foe?

TL;DR Only use a credit card if you pay the balance in full, every month. Otherwise, you will end up paying hundreds of dollars in interest charges. If used wisely, credit cards offer fantastic benefits and rewards.

Mr. Money Mustache summed up consumer debt wonderfully on his blog:

> *Consumer debt shouldn't really exist at all—it's simply a house of cards that allows impatient people to pull their consumption*

*from the future, just a teeeeny bit forward
into the present, in exchange for
spectacularly bad costs, stress, and wrecking
of lives. But because it exists and is
profitable, a huge ($1.3 trillion in 2015)
financial industry has sprung up to
originate, multiply, and churn this debt.*[10]

A credit card is one of two things:

1.   Your worst nightmare

2.   #BestFriendGoalz

The Bad

The four major credit corporations are Visa, Mastercard, Discover, and American Express. Do you ever stop and wonder how rich these companies have become because of American consumers? There's a reason these corporations are all kicking a$$.

Here's how credit cards make money from you. You go to the store and see a classy AF $250 trench coat that you must have. But then you cry a little on the inside because you have $11.85 in your checking account. Then you remember that you have a credit card, which means you can buy it right now even though you don't have $250. So, you do. Then, you make minimum payments of $15 per month until it's all paid off. Ah, the beauty of credit, amirite? Isn't $15 per month *way* better than $250 up front?

NOPE. Let's say that your credit card charges you 20% interest, which is pretty common. Guess what, Sherlock? It will take you 19 months to pay that bad boy off, and when all is said and done, you will have paid almost $50 in interest, making the total cost of that trench coat $295.37. Are you still happy with your decision? If you answered yes, go and stand in a corner and think about what you did.

Here's how credit card companies suck you in: they know that people want instant gratification. The average consumer does not consider the extra cost of using a credit card. If she does not have enough money right then and she wants to buy something, she charges it to her credit card. People are impatient and credit card companies are rich.

Credit card debt can quickly spiral out of control. Especially if you're in a situation where you *need* to buy something, instead of *want* to buy something. Flat tire? You need to get that fixed, ASAP. Don't have enough money? The easiest solution, for most people, is to charge it to their credit card. It's easy and immediate. That's why it's so important to fill up Bucket #1—so you can avoid ever being in that situation!

Humor me for a moment. What if you spend a few hundred bucks a week on your credit card, and only make minimum payments? What do you think will happen? You certainly aren't going to pay that off anytime soon. Your credit card balance will keep increasing, and the higher it gets, the longer it takes to pay off. Then your minimum payment increases. Welcome to the spiral of doom. Do you see why this is so scary? It's common! It's *easy* to get into thousands of dollars of credit card debt without even realizing it. If you are a person with no self-control, do yourself a favor and stay away from credit cards altogether. If you don't trust yourself to say *no* when you have a credit card urging you to say *yes,* stay away! Because that's when it becomes your worst nightmare.

The Good

On the flip side, credit cards can be a lovely tool if used wisely. Most of them offer perks and rewards based on dollars spent. Get this: I recently signed up for a credit card that offered some awesome travel rewards. The offer stated that if I spent $3,000 in the first three months, I would be awarded 50,000 points. I ran through my monthly expenses, and after determining that my bills, food, and gas would easily get me to that $3,000 within three months, I signed up. That's money that I would be spending anyway, so it made no difference to me whether I used a credit or debit card for it. At the end of three months, I had 50,000 points, which translated to a $500 credit. Five. Hundred. Dollars. All because I was spending money that I would normally spend.

Between my fiancé and I right now, we have over $2,000 worth of travel rewards built up from credit card sign up bonuses. Next year's international trip is on AmEx's tab. #Winning.

Credit Card Strategy

Here's the catch: I pay my credit card *in full, every month, every time.* If you pay your credit card in full, you avoid interest. Let me repeat that: if you pay your credit card in full every month, you don't ever pay a single penny in interest. Follow the pay-in-full strategy, and it's like using a debit card.

Here's the second catch: I don't *ever* buy something with a credit card that I don't have enough cash to buy that second. *Never* count on future income. It might seem like a fine idea to buy a $500 plane ticket with your credit card, even though you only have $300 in your bank account because you "know" that in two weeks you'll have the money. But it's not. What if you get fired? What if you have an emergency? Treat your credit card like a debit card, and you're golden. One more time: You only get to use the card to buy something if you have the cash.

Rewards Fo' Days

Some credit cards offer cash back rewards, meaning that you can redeem points for a credit on your statement. Some offer travel rewards, meaning that you can redeem points for airplane tickets or hotels. (Wanna know how I flew to Greece for under $200? You guessed it: a travel rewards credit card.) Some credit cards offer gift cards to hundreds of stores. I rely on the website NerdWallet.com to find and compare credit cards. You can filter based on your credit score, rewards type, fees, and more.

Credit card companies will often run promotions for a limited time. For example, many companies will entice you with up-front bonus points if you spend a certain amount, as in my previous example. Take heed: earning those bonus points is great as long as you are not going out of your way to meet the spending requirement. The last thing you want to do is go on a $700 shopping spree to earn $400 in rewards. To find the most relevant information on current promotions, Google "Best credit card rewards [year]."

Do your Research

When considering a credit card, be sure to look at the fine print for details on fees. Annual fees, foreign transaction fees, and balance transfer fees are common. I never take interest rate into account, because I pay in full every month, as will you. Read the fine print on any sign-up bonus so you know what is required for you to qualify.

My final word on credit cards: be careful and disciplined. Credit cards aren't for everyone. If you don't trust yourself to only spend within your means, then hold off for now. There's no point in risking getting into credit card debt, which is the *worst* type of debt because of the exorbitant interest rates. Don't enable yourself.

Debt—A Smorgasbord

TL;DR Other types of debt include home equity loans, personal loans, business loans, payday loans, and most commonly, mortgages. Interest rates and term lengths have the biggest impact on the total cost of your mortgage.

Mortgage

A home mortgage is a legal agreement where the bank or lender holds some rights of ownership of the house until you repay the debt with interest. You don't ever outright own your house until you've paid your entire mortgage off. If you stop making payments on your mortgage, your bank or lender can foreclose and take the property away from you. So… avoid that.

Mortgages come in all shapes and sizes. Some have fixed rates, meaning that your interest rate always stays the same. Some have adjustable rates, meaning that your interest rate can fluctuate (and usually for the worse.) Some are government-insured, like an FHA or VA or USDA loan (Federal Housing Administration, Veterans Affairs, and the United States Department of Agriculture, respectively,) and some are conventional. Mortgages can also have varying repayment periods, but the most common are 15- or 30-year terms.

Factors

The total cost of a mortgage contains two elements: principal and interest. When you take out a $200,000 loan, you're not spending only $200,000—that's just the principal amount. Add the interest cost to get your total payout.

The factors that will influence you the most over the life of a mortgage are the interest rate and term length. Let's take a look at how these two factors can impact your total payout.

First, interest rates. You and your bestie buy identical houses at the same time because #twinning. You each take out a $200,000 mortgage with a term of 30 years. Your fixed interest rate is 3.5%, and your bestie's is 4.5%. Over 30 years, if you had to take a wild guess, how much more in interest would your bestie pay?

At 3.5%, the total amount you'd pay over the life of the mortgage would be about $323,000. Your bestie would pay about $365,000. Yikes. Your bestie would pay $42,000 more than you for the same house! Isn't that crazy? A 1% difference in interest rates would cost over $40,000 in this scenario.

Now, term lengths. In another scenario, you each take out a $200,000 mortgage and your interest rates are both fixed at 4.5%. However, you have a 15-year loan, and your bestie has a 30-year loan. Now, what do you think the difference is?

The difference is even more staggering. You would pay a total of about $275,000 compared to your bestie at $365,000. So in this case, those extra 15 years are costing your friend $90,000 more in interest. (What kind of friend are you anyway, letting her do that?)

Not everyone can swing a 15-year mortgage because the payments are slightly higher. For example, the mortgage payment on a $120,000, 30-year mortgage with a 5% interest rate is $644. The same mortgage with a 15-year term length results in a payment of $949.

If you can afford the higher payment, I urge you to consider a shorter-term mortgage because not only will you pay way less in interest when all is said and done, but you will also build equity in your home a lot faster. If you can't afford the higher payment, I recommend going for a lower price range that fits a 15-year mortgage term you can afford. Buying a slightly smaller house now and paying it off faster will make it easier to buy the bigger house in the future. A shorter term length is worth consideration.

Not only does the shorter term length save you tons of moolah, but interest rates for 15-year loans are typically way lower than those for a 30-year loan. The rate for a 15-year loan could be as much as one to two percentage points lower. Add that to the impact of a shorter term length, and now we're talking an astonishing difference in total money paid out.

To give you an idea of the vast difference between the two term lengths, let's imagine a scenario. You are looking at buying a $367,000 house in Nashville. Regardless of the term length, you intend on putting 20% down, or $73,400. That leaves you with $293,600 worth of mortgage loan. Your interest rate for a 30-year mortgage would be 5.5%, and for a 15-year mortgage would be 4.4%. Check out the graphs below to get an idea of the total amount you would pay on the 30-year mortgage versus the 15-year mortgage.

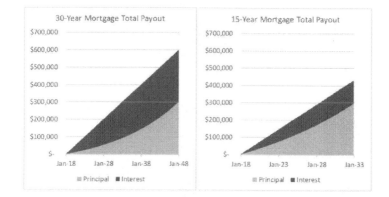

You can see that over the life of the 30-year mortgage, you will pay a total of about $307,000 in interest and about $294,000 in principal, for a total of around $600,000. Add your down payment on, and you've paid a grand total of $673,000 for a $367,000 house.

In the 15-year mortgage scenario, you will pay a total of about $108,000 in interest and about $294,000 in principal, for a total of around $402,000. With your down payment, your grand total is $475,000. The 15-year mortgage saves you almost two hundred thousand dollars!

If you wanna get real savvy without committing to a 15-year mortgage, and your loan does not have a prepayment penalty, you can always increase your monthly payments on your 30-year loan. But again: you need to make sure there are no early payoff penalties on the mortgage. Most mortgages do not have prepayment penalties, but you can't assume that. If there are no prepayment penalties, then you can pay as much as you want on top of the minimum payment each month. Paying a little extra each month could save you thousands in interest by paying the house off a few months or years sooner. So yes: you could theoretically get a 30-year mortgage and pay it off in 20 years. I recommend this strategy because it gives you the most flexibility.

By the way, all these scenarios assume you stay in or keep the house for the full term of the mortgage. That means either 15 or 30 years depending on the term length. Most people don't stay in their first or even second house for that long. I will address that scenario a little later.

There are hundreds of other factors that influence your mortgage, but those two factors—interest rates and term life—tend to make the biggest difference in your total cost. Bring these factors up with your lender and ask him or her to run multiple scenarios for you so you can apply for the ideal mortgage for your circumstances.

Amortization

"Amortization is a fun topic," said no one ever. You know what? I agree with you… I'll make it quick.

Amortization is a fancy term for the repayment schedule of a loan. An amortized loan involves regular payments consisting of both principal and interest. Ever wondered how your mortgage payment is calculated? Today is your lucky day, my friend.

Your Mortgage Payment = $hit Ton Of Interest + Tiny Dab Of Principal (at least at first)

Because of how amortization works, your first few payments are basically 99% interest and 1% principal pay down, which means you make close to zero progress paying down the principal amount for the first few years. Since so much of your payment is going towards interest, it's difficult to build equity at first. Consider the following scenario.

You buy your dream home: a sprawling ranch on the sunny West Coast on 10 acres of land, and because we're living in a fantasy world right now, you only need to take out a

$100,000 loan. Let's assume your interest rate is fixed at 6% and your mortgage term is 30 years. Using fancy amortization calculations, we know that your monthly payment will be $599.55, every month, for 30 years. Your first payment would comprise of $500 towards interest and $99.55 towards principal. Remember, interest costs are paid directly to the lender; that's how they make money. Payments towards *principal* reduce your loan balance. In other words, of your $600 payment, only $100 is actually paying down your $100,000 loan. It sort of feels like for every seven steps you take forward, you take six steps back.

By month six, your payment would comprise of $497.49 towards interest and $102.06 towards principal. You see what's happening? The total $599.55 amount stays the same each month, but most of that payment is going towards interest, or the lender, in the beginning. As time goes on, the portion going towards principal gradually increases. After six months, you've paid a total of $2,992.48, but your $100,000 loan has only decreased by $604.82. Nuts, right?

News flash: life's not fair. BTW, this amortization BS applies to every mortgage. There is no way around it. Poop.

Five-Year Rule

Want to have NO RAGRETS? Not even one letter? Then don't buy a house unless you plan on staying there for at least five years. 'Splain, Lucy. Because of amortization, you won't pay much of your principal balance off in the first few years. When you go to sell it, you might break even or lose money after paying realtor commissions and fees.

Back to our little dream home scenario that cost you $100,000: after five years, you will have paid about $36,000 total, but your principal loan amount will have only decreased by about $7,000! Just... ugh.

One would hope to buy a house, make payments, and at least recoup the amount they've paid in when they go to sell, right? Otherwise, why not rent? That's what I'm trying to tell you: owning a home for less than five years is not setting yourself up to win. After five years, in the example above, you only have $7,000 in additional equity. Typical selling fees on a $100,000 house are between $6,000 and $8,000. Best case scenario: break even.

The only thing helping you is if your home's value increases and that's never certain. To truly understand the investment, you'd need to take everything into account: not only realtor commissions and the appreciation of the house, but also the other costs of home ownership like maintenance and repairs. Regardless, don't buy a house unless you plan on keeping it for at least a few years. Otherwise, you risk losing money or breaking even, which makes it a poor use of your dollah billz.

"What if I don't intend on staying in the house for more than a couple years, but I put some serious cash into fixing it up and increasing its value? Is that a good investment?"

Many people buy a small starter home for their first house, with plans to upgrade to a larger home once they start a family. When this scenario involves making renovations to increase the value of the home, it can be a worthwhile investment. But not always. If I knew I was only going to live somewhere for a year or two, I would rent. If you won't be staying in the same place for a long time but want to buy a house, some things you can do to ensure you won't end up losing money are: buying in a buyer's market when prices are lower, putting in your time and money to fix up the house to increase its value, renting out a room to offset some of the cost, and signing up for a 15-year mortgage instead of a 30-year mortgage so you can build equity faster.

There's no black or white when it comes to home buying because everyone's situation is different. If you buy a duplex that needs some serious TLC, live in one side while renting out the other, and fix it up with your own elbow grease, it's more likely to be a profitable decision. On the other hand, if you buy a luxurious house that's already in mint condition at the peak of the real estate market and try to sell it one to two years later, you might end up with a loss.

"Hold up Rachel, don't I need a down payment to buy a house? How on earth am I supposed to save $30,000?!"

You are correct, my friend. The standard down payment requirement for a house is 20%. Buying a $150,000 house means you need 30 G's. And that's not including closing costs. So if you don't have a hefty amount in savings, I'd suggest you start there before considering buying a house.

There are ways around the 20% requirement, such as with a VA loan for veterans. My fiancé qualified for 0% down because he is a veteran of the Navy, God bless him. Even if you don't qualify for a VA loan or another government-sponsored loan or form of assistance, you might be able to get a conventional loan with only 15% down with this convenient little offering called Private Mortgage Insurance (PMI.) PMI is an extra layer of insurance that a homeowner must pay if he or she puts less than 20% down. Lenders require PMI because they take on more risk when you don't have enough equity in the house up front. PMI is the lender's way of further insuring themselves against foreclosure.

Generally, PMI goes away once you've built up 20% equity in the home. But until then, your mortgage payment will be a smidge larger because of the added cost of PMI. It's a great option in a rising interest rate environment when you don't necessarily want to wait until you have a large enough down payment. If there's anything I've learned in the world of finance, it's that there are loopholes everywhere; you just gotta look for them.

Home Equity Loans

Home equity loans, sometimes referred to as second mortgages, are loans that are secured by your real estate. There are two varieties, and to qualify for either one, you must have equity in your home. For example, if you recently bought your home using an FHA loan and only paid 3.5% down, that means you still owe 96.5% of the value of the house. In this scenario, you only have 3.5% equity, and a lender wouldn't give you a home equity loan because you cannot offer a significant enough portion of your property as collateral. However, someone who put 20% down on a home and has lived there for ten years might have closer to 30% to 40% equity in their home. This person would be eligible for a home equity loan.

The first type is an actual home equity loan, which is a one-time lump sum that is paid off over a set amount of time. You pay regular monthly payments at a fixed rate until it's paid off, exactly like a mortgage. Hence the term "second mortgage."

The second type is the Home Equity Line of Credit or HELOC. Hello, HELOC. This type works more like a credit card where you have a revolving line of credit. You can borrow up to a certain amount. As you pay off the principal, you "free up" more of the credit line, and you can use it again. For example, if you have a $10,000 HELOC, and spend $2,000 of it on a pet sloth because you have zero chill like Kristen Bell, you'd have $8,000 left to use. If you then pay back the $2,000 you have the full $10,000 of credit available again. So, it functions like a credit card. This gives you more flexibility than a fixed-rate home equity loan.

The first type, the fixed-rate home equity loan, is often used as a strategy for paying down significant credit card debt, since home equity loans have almost always had a lower interest rate than the 20% to 25% that your credit card charges. If you have significant equity in a home and are tens of thousands of dollars in credit card debt, you might consider this strategy because it could help you save tons of moolah due to the lower rate.

Other Types of Loans

We've covered the four most common types of debt: student debt, credit card debt, mortgages, and home equity loans. I'll briefly outline a few other types of debt for you:

- Personal loans. These don't have a designated purpose, meaning you can use them for anything. Like a home equity loan, some people will take out a personal loan at a lower interest rate to pay off credit debt.

- Small business loans. A small business loan is a type of loan granted to an entrepreneur to help her start or expand a business.

- Payday loans. These are the worst type of debt next to credit card debt because they are short-term, high-interest loans designed to bridge the gap from one paycheck to the next. People that live paycheck to paycheck use these to make ends meet. Do yourself a favor and pretend like you don't even know these exist. You should never use this if you follow the guidelines in this book.

- You can also borrow money from your retirement account or life insurance. P.S. Don't.

Consider that outline for educational purposes only. Remember, our goal is to lower your liabilities by paying *off* debt, not taking on new types of debt.

SECTION FOUR:
INVESTING

Say Hello to Stocks and Bonds

TL;DR Stocks > Bonds.

Oh boy, oh boy, oh boy! I have zero chill about stock market investing. IMO, it's the most fun *ever*. Incidentally, investing in the stock market is where most people seek financial advice. Questions are almost always centered around, "What do I invest in?" Buckle up buttercup, because I have a lot of information to share with you.

Definitions

First of all, what even *is* the stock market? Think of how you would define your typical outdoor flea market: a place where people can buy and sell goods. The stock market is just that but for stocks and bonds instead of goods. When stocks and bonds are bought and sold, we call that trading.

You may have heard of the Dow, the Nasdaq, or the S&P 500. These three funky dudes are all market indices, AKA benchmarks of the stock market as a whole. The Dow consists of 30 stocks, the Nasdaq of 100, and the S&P of 500. So when everyone gets all excited that the Dow is at an all-time high, it's because the Dow is an indicator of how the total stock market is doing.

A stock is a unit of ownership in a company. Buying a stock of Michael Kors means you own an itsy-bitsy piece of Michael Kors. When you own a stock, you are called a shareholder. If Michael Kors has a good year and profits go up, you "share" in those profits, meaning the value of your stock also increases.

When you invest in stock, the goal is to buy it, hold onto it for a while and let it appreciate, and then sell it for a profit.

Bonds, on the other hand, are IOUs, with *you* as the lender. When you purchase a bond from a company, you are loaning that company your money for a period of time. In return, the company pays you interest over the life of the bond. Then, when the bond matures or reaches its end date, the company pays you back your initial amount. So, you typically make money on bonds from interest.

You can also make money by trading bonds, that is, selling or buying bonds before they reach maturity. Bond prices are tied to interest rates. If interest rates go up, bond prices go down. If you sell the bond before its maturity date, there's a chance you could lose money by selling at a price less than what you paid. On the flip side, you could also potentially gain money this way; it all depends on the current interest rate environment.

With me so far? Good. Let's discuss the pros and cons of stocks and bonds since they each have a different level of risk and behave differently when the financial markets change.

Stocks: Pros

On average, stocks have consistently out-performed bonds; stocks have <u>higher returns</u>. Also, you have unlimited potential on how much you can make on an appreciating stock. It could technically go up, up, up, forever.

When you invest in stock, you become a part owner of the company. This entitles you to <u>earning dividends</u>, if offered. Dividends are profits that the company pays out to its shareholders on a regular basis.

As a shareholder, you may have <u>voting rights</u>, meaning you could have a say on who will make up the board of directors and other corporate matters. Cool, right? "Mr. Kohrs, I insist that you hire me for your Board of Directors, k thx."

Buying a stock puts you in a position of limited liability. This means that, at most, you could lose the amount you initially paid for the stock. Having <u>limited potential losses</u> while having unlimited potential gains is a huge benefit.

Stocks: Cons

Stocks tend to be <u>more volatile</u> than bonds, meaning that their prices fluctuate more. One day, your stock may be worth $100, the next day $95, and the next day $115. More volatile means more risky.

Stocks <u>do not have a guaranteed return</u>.

<u>If the company goes bankrupt, you will lose the amount that you invested</u>.

Bonds: Pros

Bonds are <u>less volatile</u> than stocks, meaning that their prices fluctuate less.

Bonds are widely used for <u>income stability</u>. Bond investors enjoy a known, reliable, and regular income payment structure.

Bonds are often used to <u>shield one's portfolio from losses</u>.

Bonds: Cons

Bonds yield <u>lower returns</u> than stocks.

<u>If the company goes bankrupt, you will lose the amount that you invested</u>.

Stocks vs. Bonds

Penny for your thoughts? Which do you think is the better investment? For me, it's stocks FTW, because I'm young and have decades until retirement. I want the greatest return possible, and I can afford to lose money in the short term, knowing that in the long term I will enjoy a much higher return.

As of this writing, most bonds are earning less than 5% interest, and the vast majority earn somewhere in the 1% to 2% range. So why would I invest in a bond and potentially lose money when I could plop it in a safe savings account and earn the same in interest?

A quick word on the relationship between risk and reward: The higher the risk, the greater the reward. The lower the risk, the lower the reward. Therefore, it makes sense that stocks are both riskier and yield higher returns than do bonds. Keep this basic principle in mind as you journey down the red carpet of investing.

If you are close to retirement, I wouldn't put all your eggs in stock. If your portfolio goes down right before retirement, it's not like you can wait a few years until it goes back up. Owning a portfolio consisting entirely of stocks five years before your planned retirement is setting yourself up to possibly take a loss, and at the worst time possible. When you near retirement, you'd want to invest in something safer and less volatile to avoid that kind of risk, which could be detrimental. Time is not on your side, which means you can't wait around for the value of your portfolio to go back up if it takes a hit right before retirement.

For the vast majority of you millennial readers, however, time is on your side, and stocks yield a higher return than their safer counterpart. Stocks bring all the boys to the yard, and I'm like, they're better than bonds.

10

Mutual Funds, Index Funds, & Which One is Your New Best Friend

TL;DR Mutual funds are pools of multiple stocks chosen by a professional. Index funds are pools of multiple stocks that automatically track to a market index. Index funds > mutual funds > individual stocks.

I'm about to blow your mind by introducing you to something better than stocks and then introducing you to something better than something better than stocks. If stocks are teenage Zac Efron in High School Musical, then mutual funds are shy but hot Channing Tatum in Step Up, and index funds are dreamy Ryan Gosling in The Notebook. Stay tuned.

First, say hi to mutual funds. Mutual funds are groovy because you can buy tons of different stocks or bonds with a single investment.

Picture a big basket of all your favorite things: Nike sports bras, Burberry perfume, Starbucks Frappuccinos, Lululemon leggings, MAC eyeliner, Crest white strips, Apple MacBooks, BMW cars, and OPI nail polish. This is giving me serious shopping spree vibes.

Now pretend that you and a bunch of other people simultaneously own all that stuff. Also, pretend that you have a professional basket manager who is in charge of picking the best goodies to go in the basket. You and the other owners pay the basket manager to monitor the goodies and make decisions on what's in and what's out.

Now imagine there are some winners and some losers in the basket. Your BMW's value goes up, but Burberry goes down. Overall though, your basket of goodies appreciates.

That, ladies and gents, is the premise of a mutual fund. The basket is the mutual fund. The goodies are the stocks that make up the mutual fund. The owners of the basket are the investors, i.e. you and whoever else buys it. The basket manager is the mutual fund manager.

As you can imagine, one of the biggest benefits of owning a mutual fund is diversification, meaning that your money is invested in tons of different companies. The risk of owning a single stock is that the company could go belly up and you'd lose all your money. It's not likely to happen with a large, well-established company, but it has in the past. Remember Lehman Brothers in 2008? Don't be that guy.

However, if you own a collection of stocks via a mutual fund, then even if one company loses value, the other stocks balance that loss out. The poor performance of one stock isn't so detrimental. In other words, the more stocks you own, the less any one of them can hurt you. Can I get an "Amen?"

"What's the catch, Rachel?" Glad you asked. Since a professional manager runs a mutual fund, you as an investor will have to pay a premium of sorts. This premium is in the form of an "expense ratio" which is a fancy term for a fee. Expense ratios are expressed as a percentage, such as 0.2% or 1.5% or 0.9%. For example, if you invest $10,000 into a mutual fund with a 2.0% expense ratio, then you pay $10,000 * 0.02 = $200 in annual fees.

The expense ratio multiplied by the total assets in the fund is the amount paid to the manager and research team, and covers administrative fees and other operating costs—it takes a lot to run a mutual fund. In short, there are higher costs associated with owning a mutual fund. Higher costs deduct from your overall return. Not cool bro.

Active vs. Passive Management

Talking about mutual funds brings me to a v important debate, in which I have v strong feelings. Here's the thing. Lots of people love the idea of an actively managed mutual fund and will happily part ways with a little extra money so a professional financial manager can make decisions for them. After all, someone that does this *full time,* for many years, will probably know a $hit ton more about which stocks to pick than the average investor, right? I mean… that's their *job.*

Not so fast. Time and time again, research has proven that *mutual funds, on average, have not significantly beaten the overall stock market.* Beating the market usually means earning an investment return greater than that of the S&P 500 index, one of the most popular benchmarks of the U.S. stock market. Let me reiterate: Research shows that the number of active mutual funds outperforming the market on a consistent basis isn't just low, it's zero.[11] #ShotsFired. Get on Google and see for yourself. So, if smart-as-hell, full-time professionals can't beat the market then what on earth are you paying them for? You wouldn't pay a personal trainer if you knew you could work out by yourself and achieve an equal result.

Don't get me wrong. That's not to say that mutual funds don't perform well. Some mutual funds outperform the overall stock market for a stretch of several years, but none have done it consistently. For this reason, I am firmly anti-mutual funds, and also anti-active management in general. Sorry not sorry.

Team Index Funds

If Ryan Gosling said to you, "Hey girl, I love it when you invest in index funds," it would be a no-brainer. Since he's not here right now (mega-unfortunate) I'll try to recreate that same effect.

So get this: an index fund is similar to a mutual fund but without the added expense of having a professional manager. An index fund owns hundreds of stocks, but its portfolio is set up to match the components of a market index such as the S&P 500. No active management is required since it's set up to automatically track something that already exists; it's passively managed. Basically, an index fund is a list of investments.

The benefit? The cost savings of having an automatic setup with no one doing research and making decisions full time gets reflected in the fund's lower fees and, therefore, passed on to the shareholders. For example, where a mutual fund might have an expense ratio of 1.2%, an index fund might have an expense ratio of 0.2%. Boom. I just earned you a 1% better return with that nugget. High fivesies.

You might think that saving a percentage point on your expense ratio doesn't make that much of a difference on your return. Allow me to prove you wrong. In the following graph, you will see what happens to a $10,000 investment over the course of ten years, with a couple different expense ratios. We assume a 10% gain per year.

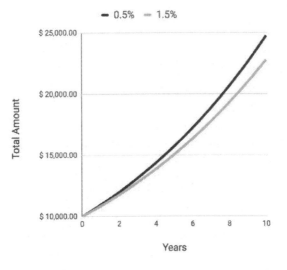

After ten years in a fund with a 0.5% expense ratio, you will have $24,758. After ten years in a fund with a 1.5% expense ratio, you will have $22,791. That's almost a $2,000 difference. If you're the type of person who likes to withdraw $2,000 in cash from the bank and then immediately be robbed, by all means, please invest in a high-expense-ratio mutual fund. If you enjoy not being robbed on a regular basis, please get your $hit together and invest in an index fund. K thx bye.

Stock market returns are unpredictable. Expense ratios are not. So, do everything you can to get that bad boy down to close to zero and enjoy the fruits of my mental labor. #AnothaDayAnothaDolla

Why ETFs are BAE

As index funds are a subset of mutual funds, exchange-traded funds (ETFs) are a subset of index funds. ETFs are the cool thing to do these days. I recommend these over regular index funds. They are passively managed like index funds, typically more convenient to trade, and often cost even less than an index fund, with some expense ratios as low as 0.03%. Cash me outside, how bow dah.

11

Four Golden Rules for Investing

TL;DR Sell when the market is high and buy when the market is low. Only invest for the long term. Don't micromanage your investments.

Investing in the stock market doesn't have to be complex. Most people are scared of the stock market because they don't understand it, and if they do understand it, they get decision paralysis because there are millions of stocks and bonds from which to pick. It's the same feeling as when you go to get your nails done, and it takes you 30 minutes to choose out a nail polish because there are so many options.

I'm here to make your life easier by giving you some rules to follow, which will help take the fear and anxiety out of investing. This is about to be the easiest part of this book. You're welcome.

Rule #1

Don't sell when the market is down. The stock market has only trended upwards in the long run. There have been times—multiple years, even—that the stock market has declined. Think of all the recessions you've experienced: the dotcom bubble in 2000 and the housing crisis in 2008, to name a couple. Recessions hit once every ten to fifteen years, like clockwork. So, your first rule of thumb is not to panic when the stock market drops. Notice I said WHEN not IF. That is because it *will* happen. And when it does, what are you NOT supposed to do? Freak out and sell all your stock. The number one worst thing you can do as an investor is selling your stock during a downturn.

Here's a fancy graph of the Dow from 1900 to 2017, proving a constant upward trend.[12]

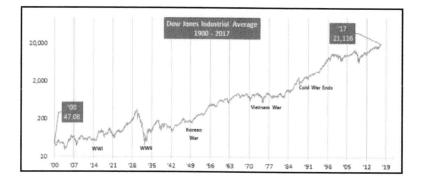

Do you remember that part in Jurassic Park where they all push back some leaves, and a T-Rex is standing right there looking at them? And the main guy goes, "Don't. Move. A. Muscle." And then everyone runs because they're all complete idiots? Yeah. Don't be the idiot that runs. #YouHadOneJob

Why is it so bad to sell during a downturn? Because selling your stock once your stock has already dropped is *locking in a loss*. "Hey, I want to buy a brand new car for $20,000, and then after a month, when it's worth way less, I want to sell it for $17,000," said no one ever. So why would you do the same thing with a stock?

I'll tell you why most people do it: sheer panic. They get caught up in everyone else's emotions, and they do what everyone else is doing when the market crashes: sell. They think that, by selling, they are preventing an even greater loss. You are bound to get caught up in the hysteria too.

Remember, when you own a stock, you only have *theoretical* gains and losses. You don't have an *actual* loss *until you sell it*. If you want it to not *become* an actual loss, hold onto it until the stock market goes back up. Just, please. I beg you. Don't sell when the market is down! The rule is to buy low and sell high. If you sell when the market is down, you are doing the opposite.

Rule #2

Along those lines, don't buy when the market is…? You guessed it! Don't buy when the market is up.

Would you rather pay full price in May for a new swimsuit, or get one on super sale in September? Would you rather pay full price for a winter coat or wait until a spring sale? Personally, I avoid paying full price for anything, ever. I only buy on sale. You can get stocks on sale too. How? Buy when the market is *down*. Stock prices will be down, and you can get them at a "discount." Buy when the market is crashing or has crashed, and sell when the market is soaring. Buy low, sell high. Cardinal Rule of Investing.

The problem is that you get caught up in everyone else's mania when the market is hot. FOMO is a thing. And its consequences are huge when you act on it while investing. The easiest way to be successful? Do the opposite of what everyone else is doing. Are your family and friends panicking and selling their portfolio because the market is going down? Awesome! This is a chance for you to buy while the stock market is having a clearance sale. Are your coworkers and neighbors bragging about their all-time-high portfolios? That's a hint that it's time to sell, not buy; you wouldn't want to pay full price, would you?

Try to have this reaction:

Stock market is down

"Woohoo big sale! C'mon everybody!"

Caveat Alert: What if you are ready to start investing but the market is doing really well? Do you wait for a dip or recession when you can buy low? Here's the deal: the timing won't ever be perfect. Please don't wait ten years to start investing. Now is better than never or later. Don't ever try to time the market. If you can avoid buying during a peak, avoid it. In general, consistent investments into the market are the way to go, even if the market is rising. If you are ready to invest, don't hold off because you're not in a recession.

As much as you can, buy low and sell high. The concept is easier said than done. You've been warned. If you follow the first two rules, then even if you invest in $hitty funds, you will probably still do better than most people. Keep that in mind. But let's lay out a couple more guidelines.

Rule #3

Rule #3 is to hold your investments for at least one year and ideally more like five, ten, or twenty years. Again, the stock market always trends upwards in the long run, but in the short run, it will be volatile. The longer you hold onto an investment, the more likely you are to win.

Confession: I began to invest in stocks when I was 18, and I have never sold any of it. And guess what? My portfolio has grown tremendously. If you look at my returns year by year, or month by month, you'll see major volatility. Lots of losses. Losses make me happy because I know that gainz are coming. Over time, my portfolio has rewarded my patience, trust, and calm demeanor with some serious growth. In the long run, you are a queen.

Another reason to avoid selling within one year is short-term capital gains tax. You will almost always have to pay taxes if you sell a stock that has appreciated in value. To ensure that you pay the lowest tax possible, hold onto the investment for at least one year. This ties back to my savings plan from Chapter Three when I told you to keep savings for purchases that are less than a year away in a high-yield savings account instead of the stock market.

Short-term capital gains are taxed at your regular tax rate. Long-term capital gains are taxed at 15% to 20% for most tax brackets and zero for the lowest two. So, here is another predictable way to increase your returns: hold onto your investments for at least a year to avoid paying higher taxes. I got strategy fo' days, yo.

Rule #4

Don't be a control freak. This is coming from the biggest Type A control freak ever, so trust me when I say I understand the struggle. If your plan is to buy some stock and analyze its performance every single day, then you should rethink your strategy. I assure you that checking in daily will cause you nothing but severe angst and buyer's remorse. Guess how often I look at my portfolio? Twice a year. I'm dead serious. Guess who has kept their cool during every small downturn we've had over the past nine years? That would be moi. The saying "less is more" applies perfectly here. Once you've decided on your strategy and bought the stock, let it be. Investing should be low-stress. Check in now and then, but for the most part, fuggedaboutit. Rule #4 is the best because if you follow it, you will almost automatically follow Rules #1 through #3. Perf.

Market Cap

To talk strategy, you need to understand a few basic terms. First, market capitalization, AKA market cap. This is a fun term to subtly drop into conversation and impress all your friends and family. Market cap is a quick way to calculate the value of a company that is trading on the stock market. It's calculated by multiplying the total number of shares by the current share price. It's also an easy way to gauge the size of the company.

For example, as of this writing, Facebook is trading at $167.24 per share, and there are nearly three billion shares. That makes its market cap almost $500 billion! Because it's over $10 billion, Facebook is classified as "large cap." Mid caps would fall between $2 billion and $10 billion, and small caps are less than $2 billion.

Because large cap companies have typically been around longer and are more established, they are seen as having less growth potential. They are safer and less volatile. Think of companies that you recognize and are familiar with: Amazon, Google, Walmart, Twitter. They are all large cap.

As the market cap size decreases, the growth potential and risk increases. The higher the risk, the greater the reward. The smallest of the small caps, with market caps of less than $50 million, are the riskiest. Think of a brand new, innovative company, that's only been around a couple years. It's likely a small cap.

Geography

Mutual funds, index funds, and ETFs are investments that hold tons of individual stocks. Many of these investments are limited to a certain part of the world. You have domestic funds, which are comprised only of companies in the United States. You also have global and international funds. This gets confusing because, in normal English speak, global and international can be used interchangeably. However, in Finance speak, these two terms mean different things.

A global fund is comprised of stocks and bonds all over the world, including the country you live in. An easy way to remember this is to picture a globe, which displays every single country.

An international fund, on the other hand, invests in stocks and bonds from all countries *except* for the one you live in.

That wraps up our vocab lesson. Keep reading to learn how to choose your investments.

The Art of Investing

TL;DR My preferred strategy is to invest 25% of my account in each of the following: domestic small cap, domestic mid cap, domestic large cap, and international. Only invest in funds with less than 0.2% expense ratios.

Disclaimer: I'm not a licensed and registered investment advisor anymore. Any investment decisions you make based on this book are done so at your own risk, and the author will not be held liable (yadda yadda yadda). Please read the full disclaimer at the end of the book.

Now that you know the rules and understand the basic terms, let's talk strategy. This will be a piece of cake, and you can celebrate by also having a piece of cake. #HaveYourCakeAndEatItToo

We are going to find some index funds and ETFs based on market cap size and geography. The proportion I use and would recommend for anyone 35 and younger is:

25% domestic small cap stock (i.e. stocks of small-sized companies in the United States)

25% domestic mid cap stock

25% domestic large cap stock

25% global or international stock blend (i.e. stocks of all-sized international companies)

Donesies. Told you it was easy, breezy, beautiful Cover Girl.

This portfolio would be considered aggressive. Why? Because it holds 100% stocks and 0% bonds. Most people invest in both, even if it is 90% stocks and 10% bonds, because of diversification. I, on the other hand, believe bonds are a poor investment, esp. in the current rising interest rate environment. So, I prefer to go balls deep in stock.

Because this scenario is so aggressive, I would only recommend it as an option to those of you who still have 25+ years until retirement. As you age, you'll want to adjust your portfolio to be slightly less aggressive. Not only are stocks more aggressive than bonds, but small cap is more aggressive than large cap. For those of you between ages 35 and 45, the following portfolio might make more sense for your timeline and goals:

15% domestic small cap stock

20% domestic mid cap stock

35% domestic large cap stock

10% domestic bonds

20% global or international stock blend

This mix is heavier in large cap stock and also incorporates bonds for a slightly less aggressive portfolio.

For those nearing retirement who want an even safer portfolio, you could adjust yours to hold less small cap, more large cap, and more bonds, or begin to sell off stocks and hold the funds in cash.

Notice that I'm not changing the domestic vs. international mix all that much. I prefer to keep most of my portfolio in domestic investments, because #Merica. I believe in our country. I'm also more familiar with our country, our stock markets, and our laws, and you gotta invest in what you know. I hold onto some global stock as a hedge. Since I'm a youngin', my portfolio is identical to the first, most aggressive scenario.

"Okay, but how do I find a good domestic small cap index fund? Halp!"

We are about to get down and dirty with some Google research so I can show you how to find the funds you want.

You're ultimately going to have to do your own research, but I will give you some guidance. You should be besties with Google by now, which is fantastic. Here are some phrases to Google:

1. "Top 10 domestic small cap index funds [current year]"

2. "Top 10 domestic mid cap index funds [current year]"

3. "Top 10 domestic large cap index funds [current year]"

4. "Top 10 international index funds [current year]"

I just googled the first phrase, clicked on the first article, and found the small cap index fund IJR, which is coincidentally my favorite fund of all time. IJR is the stock symbol that represents iShares Core S&P Small-Cap.

#BreakItDown. iShares is sort of like a brand or family of ETFs. iShares Core ETFs are a group of ETFs offered by iShare that are low-cost and tax-efficient, according to their website. iShares Core ETFs offers international and US stocks and bonds, so a little bit of everything. iShares Core S&P means that this particular ETF is tracking to an S&P 500 index. And you already know what small cap is. So what does all of this mean?

Translation: IJR is an ETF. It tracks to an S&P 500 index. It consists of domestic small-cap stocks. That's all you gotta know.

Let's check out IJR for a minute. When you look up a stock symbol, you can easily access all sorts of information. On iShares' website, you can read about the investment objective, overview, characteristics, fees, portfolio, and more. One of the most prominent sections on iShares' website is the fund's performance. Why do I give zero $hits about this section? Because past performance does not indicate future performance.

PAST PERFORMANCE HAS NOTHING TO DO WITH FUTURE PERFORMANCE!

I hope you pictured me yelling that because I was! Most newbie investors are all like, "Oh, how has this fund done in the past? 20% return?! I'M IN, CLICK." Stahp. Can you predict the future? Neither can I. So how would you know, based on a fund's past performance, how that fund will perform in the future? YOU DON'T.

For all intents and purposes, I could not care less about performance. If you are curious, as of this writing, IJR has a one-year return of 22.4%, which is insane—in a good way. I didn't even know that, and I hold a ton of this stuff! (Remember when I said I look at my portfolio twice a year? I wasn't kidding.) BRB, I need some champs because I'm a winner.

Next on iShares website are some key facts about IJR. The website lists the fund's net assets: almost $30 billion. IJR is exchanged on the NYSE, or New York Stock Exchange, as are most securities, and is tracking to the S&P SmallCap 600. Inception date: May 22, 2000.

The top ten holdings are the next section. MKS Instruments Inc, Allete Inc, and Spire Inc are the top three holdings in IJR as of this writing. You can also see the fund's investments by sector; IJR holds lots of industrial, financial, consumer discretionary, and IT stocks.

So. Much. Info. Do I take the time to read it all? Hell no, unless I need something boring to read to fall asleep at night. To me, only a couple pieces of info are relevant: market cap and expense ratio. My requirements for my portfolio are to pick certain market caps with certain geographies and to keep the expense ratio below 0.2%. IJR is a domestic small cap index fund, and its expense ratio is 0.07%. Golden!

"Rachel, if all this information and all these ratios and measurements and calculations are available, and other people take them seriously, then how could they not be important?"

I knew I smelled skepticism. We return to the active vs. passive management debate. Proponents of active management firmly believe that it's worth paying a professional to spend hours researching, calculating, projecting, and analyzing all the data out there. Proponents of passive management believe that all that work won't make you any better off. No one can beat the stock market, so why try? Pick a fund that meets your needs, and you will do as well as—or better than—the active management dudes.

I walked you through an example of a solid domestic small cap fund: IJR. Let me show you how I really do it now.

I'm Googling the next category for mid-cap stocks. I'm opening the first article. I'm writing down the top three recommendations: CIPMX, FLPSX, and, oh wait. These won't do; both of these are mutual funds. I can tell because the article talks about the fund manager and the expense ratios are over 1%. Back to Google to make sure we are getting passive index funds and not active mutual funds.

After some perusing, I see a few index funds that are recommended in more than one place: VMCIX, MDY, VO, and IWR. Now I'm Googling each stock symbol individually to get some more information. Morningstar is also a great resource to get info on stocks.

<u>VMCIX</u>: US mid cap stock fund, CHECK. Expense ratio of 0.07%, CHECK.

<u>MDY</u>: US mid-cap stock fund, CHECK. Expense ratio of 0.25%, too high. NIX.

<u>VO</u>: US mid-cap stock fund, CHECK. Expense ratio of 0.08%, CHECK.

<u>IWR</u>: US mid-cap stock fund, CHECK. Expense ratio of 0.20%, on the fence.

I'm narrowing it down to VMCIX and VO and depending on my mood I will either dig deeper or flip a coin.

You may have noticed that my two winners start with the letter V. These are both Vanguard funds. Vanguard is a corporation that offers funds with low fees in general. My portfolio is heavily invested in Vanguard and iShares funds, and Vanguard wins on lowest expense ratio nearly every time.

Following the same process above, some low-fee, domestic, large-cap index funds that meet my requirements are:

<u>VV</u>: US Large-Cap stock fund, CHECK. Expense ratio of 0.08%, CHECK.

<u>SPY</u>: US Large-Cap stock fund, CHECK. Expense ratio of 0.10%, CHECK.

A couple of international or global index funds that meet my requirements are:

<u>VWO</u>: International/Global Stock, CHECK. Expense ratio of 0.14%, CHECK.

<u>VEA</u>: International/Global Stock, CHECK. Expense ratio of 0.09%, CHECK.

With this information, a portfolio for millennials that would make me super proud would be:

25% in IJR

25% in VO

25% in VV

25% in VEA

#MicDrop. It's that easy.

Alternative Investing

The stock market isn't the only avenue that can earn you bada$$ returns. Some other vehicles in which you can invest your cash include: real estate, commodities, hedge funds, derivatives contracts, cryptocurrency, and managed futures. I do not recommend trying these out until you get your feet wet with "regular" investing. I myself have only ventured into the world of real estate investing, outside of the stock market.

If you are familiar with real estate investing, you might consider exploring that option for yourself. You can build wealth through real estate by flipping houses or holding houses. Flipping a house means buying a house, fixing it up, and reselling it for a profit. Holding a house means buying a house and renting it out to earn passive income. I'm personally a fan of obtaining rental properties for that monthly cash flow.

Another alternative investment I mentioned is cryptocurrency. Many people believe crypto is the way of the future; billions of dollars are invested in it. Cryptocurrencies are digital currencies that are designed to be secure, such as Bitcoin and Ethereum. You techy people might know what I'm talking about. Investing in crypto is the new hot thing to do. And as with any trend, one must always be cautious.

Alternative investing is riskier than the stock market. As with all investments, before you buy that rental house or crypto, do your research. These alternative investments will be much more volatile than stocks and bonds, so don't invest what you can't afford to lose, and all that jazz.

13

How to Make Your First Trade Like a Boss

TL;DR Open an account with a discount broker to save on fees. To make a trade, you'll need the ticker symbol, quantity of shares, and order type.

After "What do I invest in?" the question that I hear most often is, "Okay, but how do I physically buy a stock?" I will walk you through the process of setting up an account and making your first investment.

Discount Brokers

The easiest and cheapest way to invest in the stock market is to open up an account with a discount broker. The most difficult and expensive way to invest is to open an account with a financial advisor. That's because a financial advisor is an actual person that you pay to do all of this for you. Which doesn't work for us because A) it's hard to find a financial advisor that you like and trust, and B) What did I tell you about the importance of keeping fees low?

For this reason, you will be opening an account with a discount broker. A broker is a person or institution that buys and sells goods for others. In this case, the goods are securities. A discount broker charges wayyyyy less when people make trades on the market because they don't provide investment advice. Which is fine because you bought this book to enable yourself, remember?

Examples of discount brokers are Scottrade, TD Ameritrade, Charles Schwab, Vanguard, and Fidelity, to name a few. Oh, and BTW, this is all done online. Can I get a #HellYeah?

Remember, our goal is to pay the lowest fees possible when investing. Fees are often charged by way of "trade commissions," which are one-time fees you pay whenever you buy or sell a security. A typical low-cost trade commission might be anywhere from $5 to $8 per trade for index funds or ETFs. Some brokers have account minimums and other rules, so be sure to read the fine print.

Fidelity and Vanguard, two of the most popular discount brokers, both offer a few funds for which they do not charge transaction or trade commissions. For Fidelity, these funds are iShares and Fidelity ETFs. Vanguard's commission-free funds are Vanguard ETFs. Consider this logic: if your goal is to save the most money on fees, and you decide to invest in Vanguard ETFs, you should probably open an account at Vanguard. I personally use Fidelity, because that's where my company's 401(K) is held, so it's more convenient for me. Many discount brokers offer rewards for opening an account, so be sure to take advantage of any promotional offers.

Opening an Account

Let's say you decide to open an account at Vanguard. Congrats! You're on your way to making your first investment. Opening the account is the easy part. Go to Vanguard.com, and navigate to their website for personal investors. Look for an option to open an account. You will be asked how you plan to fund the account: A transfer from your bank or other Vanguard account, a rollover from an employer plan, or a transfer from a financial institution. Answer and proceed. Now you will be asked to register on Vanguard.com. Either log in if you already have an account, or register.

Select an individual account for just you, or joint if it's for you and your SO. You'll be asked to input all sorts of info like your name, birthdate, and SSN. Then you'll "establish funding" using your bank routing and account number. You will E-Sign and then register for online access. Vanguard's forms are pretty easy and self-explanatory, so this should all take ten minutes tops. Note that it will take a couple days for your funds to move over. Once the cash is there, you can start investing!

Vanguard provides a helpful little summary of what it takes to open an account. Here is a screenshot from their website.

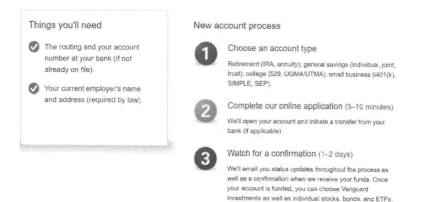

The account opening process is pretty similar for each discount broker, but if you ever get held up, don't hesitate to call the customer service number.

Making a Trade

You are one step away from becoming an investor! Now that you have opened and funded a brokerage account, you can place a trade (buy or sell stock) from the comfort of your computer screen. To make a trade, you'll need three things: ticker symbol, quantity, and order type. Keep in mind that the market is only open from 9:30 am to 4:00 pm EST, Monday through Friday.

When you are ready to buy an index fund, you can place the order by yourself from the "trade" screen of your brokerage account. Each fund is represented by a ticker symbol, and this symbol is what you'll enter in to specify what you want to buy. Below is an example of what I see in my own fidelity account when I am placing an order.

+ Cash Available to Trade	$128.48
Settled Cash	$128.48
	AS OF 09/06/2017 6:22 PM ET

Transaction Type   **Symbol**

Stocks/ETFs ▾

Trading Session
◉ Standard Hours   ○ Extended Hours ?

Action   **Quantity**

Select ▾

Order Type

Select ▾

Time in Force

Day ▾

Cancel   **Preview Order**

You'll also need to know how many shares to buy. If you have $2,000 of available and VTI is priced at $200, you can buy ten shares. Plan how you want to allocate your money before you place any orders so that you can calculate how many shares of each fund you'll need to purchase. Don't over-allocate your money; it's better to have a small portion leftover as cash.

Next is order type. The first and most common type of order is a market order. This means that the stock will be bought or sold at the best available price at that point in time, i.e. at the moment you click "Place Order." Buying and selling are not always instantaneous. The order can take a few seconds or minutes to go through, meaning that you may get a slightly different price than the one you originally saw.

For that reason, some consumers choose to use a limit order, which tells the broker only to buy or sell the shares if you can get $XX price or better. The catch is that your order could expire before the stock ever gets to that price. I have only ever used market orders, and I urge new investors getting started to do the same.

You'll also need to input "Time in Force," which indicates how long the order will remain active before it is executed or expires. This should automatically default to "Day" which means that it will be canceled if it does not execute by the closing of the trading day. If for some reason your market order does not execute by 4:00 pm EST, you'll need to place it again the next day. This has never happened to me, and I doubt it will happen to you, so don't fret. The other options, "On the Open" and "On the Close," do not apply to you right now.

You might see a couple other fields when you are filling in your order. One of them is price, which is only used when you're doing a limit order. You might see fields for expiration, special instructions, and routing. New investors should ignore these fields for now.

⊕ Cash Available to Trade		$128.48
Settled Cash		$128.48
	AS OF 09/06/2017 6:22 PM ET ↻	

Transaction Type　　　**Symbol**

Stocks/ETFs ▾	IJR

ISHARES CORE S&P SMALL CAP (IJR)

69.05 [+]

⬆ 0.21

Prospectus ⧉

Bid	66.54 x 1
Ask	70.88 x 5
Vol	1,925,915

AS OF 09/06/2017 4:10 PM ET ↻

Trading Session

◉ Standard Hours　　　◯ Extended Hours ⑦

Action　　　**Quantity**

Buy ▾	10

Order Type

Market Order ▾

Time in Force

Day ▾

Cancel　　**Preview Order**

To keep it simple, use a market order. Enter your ticker symbol and quantity, review all the information, take a deep breath, and, *drum roll, please…* click the Place Order button. Woohoo! You've officially bought your first stock! Pop open some bubbly to celebrate and shoot me an email at moneyhoneyrachel@gmail.com so I can celebrate with you too. Cheers to you, my dear friend!

14

Retirement—A New Definition

TL;DR The two most common types of retirement accounts are the 401(K) and IRA. Either account can be set up as traditional or Roth, and you will decide which type based on your current vs. future expected earnings. Think of retirement as the moment at which your passive income exceeds your expenses.

Once upon a time, there was a widely held belief that if you worked hard for 40 years, you'd be able to retire at age 60 and spend your remaining years traveling, golfing, lounging by the pool, and living a life of luxury. However, more and more people are catching onto the fact that this is a BIG,

FAT, LIE. If you are still holding out hope, then snap out of it! Ain't nobody got time for that sort of nonsense.

Your end-of-life years are your most expensive. You have to pay for medical expenses and long-term care on top of what it takes to get by, which adds up to a lot these days. What sucks more is that we are living longer. Kidding, it's spectacular. But longer life expectancy means more years that you have to support yourself in retirement. What used to be a ten-year retirement is now twenty or thirty years long! That's a whole lotta time to live off your nest egg.

More often than not, people retire at age 60 or 65 only to go back to the workforce a few years later because $hit is expensive. A new "retirement number" is circulating. That number is $2 million. Experts are saying that millennials will now need to save $2 million for retirement.[13] TWO MILLION DOLLARS. That has six zeroes, in case you didn't know. One does not simply save $2 million in her lifetime.

If you have 30 years until retirement, take a wild guess at how much you need to save per year to have $2 million? TAKE A GUESS, MY SAD LITTLE FRIEND. Assuming a reasonable 6% return, you'd need to save *twenty thousand dollars per year*. This is not a drill.

Conclusion: although retirement is far off, saving for retirement is an *immediate and urgent* matter. You must save a ton of money. You must start saving a ton of money *now*. Or accept that you either won't be able to retire when you want, or you will live a drastically different (read:

lesser) lifestyle. Saving twenty thousand dollars per year, or $770 per paycheck, for thirty years is no easy feat.

Allow me to remind you that no one knows how much money they need for retirement. $2 million is a ballpark number based on averages and who knows what. Everyone's situation is different. Some people could get by with a lot less and some need way more. You can find a million retirement calculators online and play around with assumptions to get an idea for your particular situation. Entire books have been written on how much money you need to retire. Go get 'em, tiger.

A New Way to Define Retirement

How do you define retirement, anyhoo? Most of us think of retirement as the moment at which we have enough money accumulated to live off of until we die. Another way of saying this is the moment at which we can stop working because we have enough moolah to sustain our lifestyle.

I prefer to think of retirement in a different way. You ever heard of passive income? Passive income, my friend, is income that is passively earned—who woulda thought? Unlike active income, earned from a typical job, you don't have to "work" or "clock hours" to earn passive income. Passive income comes from revenue streams such as rental property income, royalties on book sales and music sales, and dividends from stock. These revenue streams are self-sustaining. You may have to put in the work up front to set up the revenue stream, like writing a book, but once that product is created, it can earn income forever and ever.

My fiancé and I currently own two rental properties. One makes about $500/month in profit, and the other makes about $600/month in profit. There are some small tasks like maintenance and upkeep on these properties, but otherwise, I don't have to lift a finger, and the rental income comes in like clockwork every month. How would your life change if you made an extra $1100 per month without working?

How would your life change if you made $5,000 per month in passive income? Would that replace your income from your full-time job? If so, then you would be RETIRED, congratulations!

In short, I define retirement as the moment at which your passive income covers your expenses. If you're generating enough passive income that you no longer need to work, then you are retired. Fact. What's exciting about this concept is that you don't have to wait 40 years until you have accumulated enough money to stop working. You can work on generating passive income streams NOW so that in five or ten years, you can retire!

I could write an entire book on how to generate passive income streams, but I'll save that for my sequel ☺. For now, please read MJ Demarco's book, "Fastlane Millionaire." It will forever change the way you think about retirement.

401(K)

The 401(K) is perhaps the most well-known term that has to do with retirement savings. A 401(K) plan is offered by an employer and allows workers to invest part of their paycheck directly into the plan. There are all sorts of rules, but here's the #NeedToKnow:

- The employee gets to control how the money is invested. Most plans offer a variety of mutual funds or index funds.

- Many employers make matching or partial contributions. For example, your employer may offer to match the first 3% that you contribute. If you make $100,000 and you contribute 10% per year to your 401(k), the employer would match the first 3% or $3,000 and throw that in there too. Free money! This is the biggest perk of the 401(K).

- Vesting defines the amount of time you must work for your company before you are "entitled" to any employer contributions. #MoodKiller

- There are limits on how much you can contribute. In general, employees can contribute $18,000 at most per year.

- You have to wait until you're 59 ½ years old to withdraw money. If you don't wait, you'll have to pay a ten percent early withdrawal penalty. So, plan on waiting.

That's the gist. There are other employer-sponsored plans that are similar to the 401(K). For example, the 403(b) is a retirement plan for certain employees of public schools or non-profits. A 457 plan is available for most government employees in the United States.

FYI, you own your 401(K) and all the contributions you make to it, but that's not always the case for employer contributions. A nifty concept called vesting outlines when you are entitled to employer contributions and when you are not. For example, if you've worked at your company for less than a year and then quit, many companies will withdraw the employer contribution from your 401(K). These policies are in place in part to encourage loyalty and lower employee turnover. Vesting requirements differ for each company so you should speak with HR regarding the rules for your own account. To clarify: your own contributions are always your own, but vesting rules dictate when the employer contributions officially belong to you.

What happens to the account when you leave your employer? Not much. It remains a 401(K) and you retain access and ownership. You don't have to do anything, but doing nothing is usually not your best choice. That's because after you move on from your employer, your investment options will continue to be restricted to what's available in your plan.

Your best option is to roll it over into an IRA. That's where the term "rollover IRA" comes from; it's a 401(K) that has been transitioned into an IRA. Speaking of...

IRA

An IRA is an individual retirement *arrangement,* according to the IRS. Most people think it stands for an individual retirement *account,* and it doesn't matter, but you can now be that annoying jerk that corrects everyone around you with your meaningful and profound knowledge.

Anyone with earned income can open an IRA, but there are rules and restrictions. For example, the "no-withdrawals-before-age-59 ½" rule also applies to an IRA. The max contribution for an IRA is way less than a 401(K); for 2017, you can only contribute $5,500 (with certain exceptions.)

Allow me to clarify that an IRA isn't a type of investment; it's a type of account. You can't ask, "Yo, what interest rate can I get on an IRA these days?" It's not a high-yield savings account that pays a specific interest rate. It's a vehicle in which to save money for retirement, same as a 401(K). You can open an IRA with cash and leave it or you can invest the cash in the stock market.

There are several different types of IRAs. Here are a few of them:

- Individual IRA: Standard type of IRA; Any individual can open.

- SEP IRA: Simplified Employee Pension. A SEP is set up by an employer for the benefit of its employees. All SEP contributions are made by the employer. SEPs are mostly used by self-employed individuals

or small business owners. They have higher
contribution limits.

- <u>SIMPLE IRA</u>: Savings Incentive Match Plan For
  Employees. Another retirement plan that is
  established by an employer, but this time, eligible
  employees can also contribute. It has higher
  contribution limits.

- <u>Self-Directed IRA</u>: A special IRA that allows for
  alternative and normally riskier investments (Think:
  real estate investing.)

Traditional vs. Roth

Almost all retirement accounts offer tax benefits. The tax
benefit depends on whether the account is a traditional or
Roth account. IRAs offer both options and most 401(K)s
these days do too.

Traditional and Roth accounts differ on tax treatment. In
general, contributions to a traditional retirement account
are tax-deductible. You get a tax benefit up front when you
contribute to a traditional IRA, and then funds grow tax-
deferred, meaning that you don't pay income taxes on
interest, dividends, or capital gains until you take a
withdrawal. Basically, you are pushing your taxes owed into
the future.

A Roth account is the exact opposite. Contributions are *not*
tax deductible, but funds grow tax-free. So you pay taxes

like normal up front, but you don't pay taxes when you withdraw your funds later.

Because this is confusing AF, let's look at a real-life example. Bada$$ boss lady Janice makes $50,000 as an accountant. She's trying to decide whether to open a traditional or a Roth IRA. She would like to contribute $5,000 this year.

Let's say she goes for the traditional IRA. Because Janice meets certain requirements, she is eligible to take a tax deduction for the full amount of $5,000. This means that her taxable income is reduced by $5,000 to $45,000, so that's $5,000 less income that she has to pay taxes on. If Janice pays 30% in taxes, she is saving $1,500 in taxes.

Fast forward to 35 years later when she is retiring and making her first withdrawals. Withdrawals from traditional IRAs are taxed as regular income based on your tax bracket for the year in which you make the withdrawal. When Janice is retired, she's in a lower tax bracket: 25%. When she withdraws that $5,000 during retirement, she will have to pay taxes of $1,250. In this scenario, the traditional IRA works in her favor *because her tax bracket during retirement is LOWER*. Janice saved $1,500 up front and paid $1,250 during retirement for a net tax savings of $250. We can conclude that you are better off in a traditional IRA or 401K if you expect to be in a *lower* tax bracket when you retire.

On the other hand, bada$$ boss lady Claire works as a mechanical engineer and makes $60,000 per year. She also wants to contribute $5,000 this year into an IRA. Let's say she goes for the Roth IRA. Her taxable income this year will still be $60,000 since she doesn't get a tax deduction for contributing to a Roth IRA. However, later on, when she's retired, she doesn't have to pay any taxes.

Let's say Claire is in a much higher tax bracket during her retirement. If this is the case, she has saved money overall from a tax perspective by investing in a Roth. Since her tax bracket is *higher* in retirement than it was when she was contributing to the Roth IRA, the Roth IRA was the right choice.

To sum it all up: if you expect to be in a lower tax bracket during retirement than you are now, the traditional IRA will be more advantageous. If you expect to be in a higher tax bracket during retirement than you are now, the Roth IRA is generally the better choice.

"Okay, so what?" you ask. *"How does this help me right now?"* Excellent point. Do any of us know what our tax bracket will be in retirement? No. Because no one can read the future. Yes, you can hypothesize, you can make assumptions, you can plan for a certain outcome, but that doesn't mean that your life will play out that way. It's impossible to know what your life will be like during retirement. Because of that, it's difficult to know for sure whether you should open a traditional or Roth IRA.

Because of certain eligibility restrictions, you might not even qualify for the up-front tax deduction that comes with a traditional IRA. It depends on how much you make and whether your employer offers a retirement account. For instance, if you're making $300,000 as a neurosurgeon at a hospital that offers a 403(b), then a traditional IRA won't do $hit for you, because you won't qualify for the tax benefit. You should go for the Roth IRA where you can reap the tax benefits later on. Look into your eligibility first because that might make your decision easy.

Or you might be like me, and function under the assumption that you will be one rich MF during retirement and therefore in a much higher tax bracket. #DareToDream right? Because I am optimistic, I invest solely in Roth IRAs and Roth 401Ks.

Maybe you're having a tough year financially, and you can take any break you can get. Maybe you were laid off in the same month that your car broke down, in the same month that you got robbed, in the same month that you've had to financially support your sibling. Maybe you could use any tax break possible, ASAP. In that case, why not take advantage of the traditional IRA's tax deductions? I say go for it. I'm all about manipulating the tax system to better your current situation!

The point is, as I've said many times, there's no one size fits all. Everyone is living a different set of circumstances. Be sure to consider all factors before deciding what type of retirement account to open.

SECTION FIVE: TAXES & INSURANCE

15

Taxes Don't Have to Be Taxing

TL;DR Your taxable income minus deductions equals your adjusted gross income (AGI.) Use your tax brackets and your AGI to determine your gross tax liability. Subtract tax credits to get your final tax liability. Compare this amount with how much you withheld the previous year to see if you'll get a refund or if you'll owe. If your refund is large, consider adjusting your withholdings so you do not continue to loan your money to the government interest-free.

New tax regulations are enacted every single day. Wanna know how many pages were in the federal tax code in 2016? *Seventy-four thousand six hundred eight pages.*[14] 74,608! Once upon a time, the tax code was less than 500 pages. In the past thirty years alone, it's grown by almost three times in length. For Pete's sake, we have an entire industry dedicated to helping people with their taxes. We pay CPAs hundreds of dollars now to fill out hundreds of pages of tax forms. Thanks, government, for making this unnecessarily complicated.

Have no fear! I am here to help you sift through the hideousness that is the tax code. In this chapter, you'll learn only the need-to-know: how taxes work, how refunds are calculated, and how to adjust your withholdings.

Tax Brackets

First of all, here in the grand old USA, we have a progressive tax rate, meaning that people who have higher incomes pay a higher proportion of their money to the government. Tax brackets in the United States range from 10% to 39.6% percent in 2017:

Rate	Taxable Income Bracket
10%	$0 to $18,650
15%	$18,650 to $75,900
25%	$75,900 to $153,100

28%	$153,100 to $233,350
33%	$233,350 to $416,700
35%	$416,700 to $470,700
39.6%	$470,700+

People fail to understand that it's not like, "Oh I make $20,000 so I pay 15% of $20,000 which is $3,000." Wrong. What actually happens is that you pay 10% on the first $18,650 (as in the tax bracket above) and then you pay 15% on the next $1,350.

$$\$18,650 \times 10\% = \$1,865$$

$$\$1,350 \times 15\% = \$202.5$$

$$\text{Total tax owed} = \$2,067.50$$

This means that your *effective* tax rate is $2,067.50 / $20,000 = 10.3%. Make sense? Botta bing, botta boom. By the way, this is only for federal taxes. Not state and local.

How Taxes Are Calculated

Here's the high-level: First, you calculate your taxable income by starting with your total income and subtracting out deductions, adjustments, exemptions, and so forth. Then you calculate your tax liability by using the current-year tax brackets, like we did previously. Next, subtract out credits to get your net tax liability. Finally, based on how much you already paid due to paycheck withholdings, you either owe more to the gov or you get a refund.

Now, for the nitty-gritty, if you so desire. Here are the specific steps to determine your federal income taxes.

First, determine your gross taxable income. This will include wages, tips, commission, alimony, interest, capital gains, and more. Child support, gifts, workers comp, and some other categories are non-taxable income, so those would not be included.

Next, calculate your adjusted gross income (AGI). Your AGI equals your gross taxable income minus any "adjustments," which are defined by the IRS. Examples of adjustments include student loan interest (holla!), contributions to a traditional IRA, and tuition and fees.

Next, subtract deductions from your AGI. When calculating your deductions, you can either take the standard deduction or itemized deductions. The standard deduction is a preset amount each year that the IRS allows you to claim, whereas itemized deductions are a detailed list of your actual deductions. You would take whichever is higher. Typical deductions include medical and dental expenses, personal property taxes, home mortgage interest, and gifts to qualified charities. This is where homeowners will pat themselves on the back because of all the fun tax deductions they get.

After you've subtracted deductions from your AGI, subtract exemptions. You can claim one exemption for yourself if no one can claim you as a dependent. You can also claim exemptions for each dependent that you have. Unfortunately, pets do not count as dependents.

So at this point, you have subtracted adjustments, deductions, and exemptions from your gross income to get your taxable income. Now you'll do all the fancy math with the tax table to calculate your gross tax liability.

Next is to calculate credits. An important distinction between deductions and credits: tax credits provide a dollar-for-dollar reduction of your income tax liability. This means that a $1,000 tax credit saves you $1,000 in taxes. On the other hand, tax deductions *lower your taxable income*. Therefore, a tax credit is always worth more than a dollar-equivalent tax deduction. Common credits include the Child Credit, Dependent Care Credit, and Earned Income Credit. So now you subtract tax *credits* from the gross tax liability which gets you to your final net tax liability.

The final step is to determine the taxes that you have already paid for the year, which is the sum of all the money withheld from your paychecks. If you've withheld MORE than your final tax liability, you will get a refund of the difference. If you've withheld LESS than your final tax liability, you must pay the difference.

Here's the overall formula:

	Gross Income
less:	Deductions for Adjusted Gross Income (AGI)
	AGI
less:	Greater of Itemized or Standard Deduction
less:	Exemption(s)
	Taxable Income
times:	Tax Rate (using tax tables)
	Gross Tax Liabilitiy
less:	Tax Credits
	Net Tax Liability

There's a lot going on there, so let's try out a real-life scenario. I'm going to give you all the deets, and you're going to calculate the tax refund or tax owed. If you come up with the correct answer, reward yourself with tacos and margs.

It's 2017, and Monica is a chef in New York with a $55,000 salary. On top of her salary, Monica also earned $500 in interest from her savings account and received a $1,000 cash gift from her mom on her birthday. She contributed $1,500 to a traditional IRA. Monica will be taking the standard deduction, which is $6,350 for single taxpayers in 2017. A total of $6,389.89 was withheld the previous year from her paycheck for taxes. Will Monica get a federal tax refund or owe money, and how much?

Insert Jeopardy song

Here's a line-by-line table that lays out the entire calculation.

Gross Income	$55,500	Salary plus interest (Mom's gift doesn't count)
Adjustments	$1,500	A $1,500 contribution to traditional IRA
AGI	$54,000	Gross Income minus adjustments
Standard Deduction	$6,350	2017 standard deduction for single filer
Exemption(s)	$4,050	2017 personal exemption for single filer
Taxable Income	$43,600	AGI minus deductions minus exemptions
Gross Tax Liability	$5,607.50	First $18,650 x 10% plus the next $24,950 x 15%
Tax Credits	$0	No tax credits
Total Withheld	$6,389.50	Total amount withheld from paychecks
Tax Refund/Due	$782	Total withheld minus gross tax liability: REFUND

Because Monica's withholdings were greater than her gross tax liability, she receives a refund of $782. I would recommend that she adjust her withholdings so she doesn't receive such a large refund. Keep reading (while enjoying your tacos and margs) to find out why.

Tax Refunds & Withholdings

Are you one of those people who gets excited about your tax refund? Do you have family and friends that look forward to Tax Day because they're expecting a big chunk of change? STOP IT. RIGHT MEOW. To quote über-conservative blogger Matt Walsh:

> *Every year, I endure the spectacle of people celebrating their 'refunds' as if it's a winning scratch-off ticket. But there's nothing to celebrate. You should actually be angry about your refund, and I'll explain why. Your 'refund' is, for a lot of you, not a sudden, magical windfall, but simply the government paying back what it owes you. Your 'refund' means that the government took more in taxes than it was entitled to, then held onto this compulsory 'loan,' and finally paid it back without interest.*
>
> *And they only give it back if you come to them and ask for it back. If you enter some numbers in wrong, or you forget about a couple of forms or whatever, they'll keep the money. They'll keep it forever if you let them.*

Compare that to how they treat you if you owe them. You better believe there will be penalties and late fees on that money, and the fact that you didn't know you owed them will not be an acceptable excuse. It's only acceptable for them. But you are not them.

Yes, I understand you're glad to have your money back, but let's not jump for joy and fall on our knees thanking the State for giving us back our own money without interest. And if you get a ton of money back in a refund, that's even more money that you lost because it could have been accruing interest in savings, or you could have invested it. All in all, you got screwed. I hate to be a killjoy, but we should all understand how taxes work and what the government is actually doing.[15]

Matt Walsh, FTW, ladies and gents. (Disclaimer: Matt Walsh has divisive opinions, and his views do not represent my own. I think he nails it with his perspective on tax refunds, but I cannot say they same for much else.)

Each paycheck, the government withholds some of your money based on some forms you filled out about your income, dependents, and so forth. Come April, when you actually DO your taxes, you'll find out how much you DID owe the government for the last calendar year. If you owe them *more* than what was withheld, you have to pay them. If you owe them *less* than what was withheld, they refund you *your own money*. And they don't even pay you interest! If you're thinking, "What a freakin' scam!" then you have seen the light, my friend.

This is why it is so important to fill out your withholdings form correctly. I'm pissed when I get a big fat refund. That's like saying, "Here government, take $3,000 of my own money interest-free for like a year. You can pay me back in April!" WHO WOULD DO THAT? I'm not in the business to lend anyone money, let alone interest-free. So, you better believe I'm going to withhold *just* enough that I receive a minimal refund, if at all. This past year I owed in state taxes and received a small refund in federal taxes, so it all netted out to about a $300 refund. That's close to perfect in my book.

If you aren't enthused about loaning the government your money interest-free, allow me to teach you about your withholdings form, which is only applicable for employees of a company.

Form W-4

You can control how much your employer withholds from your paycheck using a Form W-4. This form allows you to determine your withholding allowances and can be amended at any time. The more withholding allowances you claim, the less the employer withholds. You likely filled out a W-4 when you first started working for your employer. The IRS has a nifty little tool that helps you calculate how much should be withheld and whether you should submit an updated W-4 to your employer. Check it out at https://www.irs.gov/individuals/irs-withholding-calculator.

If you are self-employed, nothing is automatically withheld from your paycheck. To avoid a HUGE tax bill come April, you should be imposing your own withholding systems. I sold Cutco as an independent contractor to pay for my college education, and when I filed taxes that first year it was like someone punched me in the gut. I owed an enormous tax bill because of my earnings and because nothing was being automatically withheld from my paycheck. Don't make my mistakes! You can Google online self-employment tax calculators to get an idea of how much you will owe, and then regularly set aside this money throughout the year so it doesn't come as a total shock in April.

Should I Get a CPA?

I've done my taxes every year so far using TurboTax. I've always been either self-employed or employed by a corporation. I'm also single with no kids so my returns are relatively straightforward. However, now that I've invested in real estate and run a couple other businesses, I will use a CPA to do my taxes. My opinion is that for a straightforward return, TurboTax is super valuable. When you get into estates, owning your own corporation, real estate investing, and complex tax scenarios, a CPA will be worth the money. If you're self-employed and not organized about keeping your receipts and logging your miles, you might also want to consider hiring a CPA.

Don't Be Stupid; Be Insured

TL;DR If you have no dependents, you do not need life insurance. If people are dependent on you financially, then term life insurance is better than whole. Long-term disability insurance is sometimes more important than life insurance.

What is life insurance?

Life insurance is a contract with an insurance company. You pay the company regular payments, and in return the company provides a lump-sum payment, AKA death benefit, to your beneficiaries when you die. Rosy.

A common misconception is that everyone needs life insurance. Let me #mythbust this for you. First, consider the purpose of life insurance. Think about your parents. Maybe one of them stayed at home to raise you while the other worked. What happens if the working parent suddenly dies? The stay-at-home parent is left without income. Meaning he or she has no immediate way to continue to support the kids. But if the working parent had life insurance, then upon his or her death, the stay-at-home parent would receive a sum of money to sustain the family for a length of time. This is hugely beneficial because the kids are dependent on the stay-at-home parent, and the stay-at-home parent is dependent on the working parent. Life insurance eliminates the risk of losing an income stream due to the death of that working parent. Life insurance means that your family is provided for no matter what happens to you. It's incredibly important to have *if* people are dependent on you.

Long story short: you only need life insurance if you have people that are dependent on you financially. Or, you know, if you have a pet that you love. So, for all of you single people who have no kids or parents who depend on you financially, enjoy not paying life insurance premiums for now.

Your need for life insurance will increase with your age and responsibilities. The amount of insurance you buy should reflect the standard of living you wish to assure your dependents. You'll calculate that amount while taking into account any assets that are already available, Social security benefits, the value of your home, and any other cash on hand. You'll also want to consider all the costs that the death benefit will need to cover; not only enough money to replace your current income, but also to cover future education costs, funeral costs, debts, and even the rising cost of goods due to inflation.

Even if you do have dependents, you may not need insurance. If you're a trust fund baby, for example, and have millions of dollars, then you might opt for no life insurance even if you have kids because you already have enough $$$ to sustain them for the rest of their lives.

Another common misconception is that if you *do* have dependents, you need to buy life insurance for the rest of your life. Let's think this through. Phoebe is a single, working mom who has one ten-year-old daughter. Phoebe clearly needs insurance because her daughter is dependent on her to survive. But does that mean she needs insurance for the rest of her life? Maybe, maybe not. Wouldn't one expect that by age 25, her daughter would be financially self-sufficient? If so, Phoebe only needs life insurance for the next 15 years of her life, to bridge that gap for her daughter. As you can see, life insurance needs vary for each situation.

As with most things, there is an exception to the rule. Some individuals opt for a life insurance policy even if they have no dependents, to cover the expense of a funeral in case of death.

Your company may offer life insurance. I get a free life insurance policy through work even though I do not need it. Learn about the life insurance policies provided at work before looking into purchasing any additional policies.

Term vs. Whole

There are two major types of life insurance: term and whole. As in Phoebe's scenario, term life insurance is designed to provide financial protection for a specific period of time. Traditionally, the premium payment amount stays the same during the entire period of coverage. Once the period ends, you sometimes have the choice to extend the coverage but usually for a substantially higher rate. Term life insurance is generally less expensive than whole life insurance.

Another scenario when someone might use term life is caring for elderly parents. Let's say your parents are in their nineties and are dependent on you financially. If something happens to you, they're screwed. You might opt to get life insurance for a five- or ten-year period to safeguard them against your death.

Term life insurance is as basic and inexpensive as it gets and more than adequate for most situations.

Whole life insurance provides lifetime coverage, which translates to higher premium payments. Whole life has insurance and investment components. The insurance component pays a predetermined death benefit when you die. The investment component builds an accumulated cash value that you can borrow against or withdraw. Earnings accumulate tax-free or tax-deferred. With this type of insurance, you can accumulate wealth over time.

The biggest disadvantage of whole life insurance is the cost, which will always exceed a term policy with the same death benefit, sometimes by thousands of dollars a year. Another downside is that you normally don't have a say in what the cash value component is invested in; that's up to the life insurance company.

Long-Term Disability Insurance

When you don't have insurance, can you think of something that would suck more for your kids than your death? I can! That would be if you were paralysed and could no longer care for yourself. Not only does your family lose your stream of income, but *you* become a financial burden on *them.* For the rest of your life. Do you see how having no long-term disability insurance could be a hundred times more detrimental to your family than having no life insurance?

Long-term disability insurance helps replace some of your income for an extended period when you cannot work at all or can only work part-time because of disability. This insurance is usually provided by employers, but if you want additional coverage, you can purchase an individual plan from an insurance agent.

When I was a little kid, I was outside playing with friends while my dad was working on a high-reaching ladder to build us a rockin' playhouse. While bragging to my friends about this upcoming attraction, I idiotically decided to sit down on the bottom rung of the ladder while he was working. My weight caused the ladder to shift slightly, and before I knew it, my dad was tumbling 15 feet to the ground, sharp tools in hand. It was horrifying. Luckily, he was fine. But what if he had broken his back? (What if *I* had broken his back?!) I'M SORRY DAD. At the time, my mom was staying at home raising my two sisters and me. If my dad was out of work for six months recovering, what would they have done?! This is why long-term disability insurance is important.

Even though most employers offer these plans, chances are they don't offer a large enough benefit to sustain you and your family if you ever get into this situation. Most plans only replace a portion of your current income—typically 50% to 70%—and only for a certain period of time. In reality, you may need all of your current income replaced for the rest of your life in a worst-case scenario.

Pros of long-term disability include that there are no restrictions on how you can use the money, and the benefit is tax-free. Cons are that if you never become disabled, it's not like you get the money you paid back. Long-term disability insurance works like term life insurance where if

XX happens, you get the benefit. If XX doesn't happen, you don't get the benefit and you don't get your money back. That's the premise of insurance.

You'll need to weigh the benefits against the costs to decide what's right for you, but nothing beats speaking to an expert. Find an insurance agent you can trust to review your insurance situation and make recommendations.

SECTION SIX: STRATEGY

17

The Money Honey Plan: 7 Simple Steps

TL;DR There are 7 Steps to financial freedom. The first three can be completed in one day. Don't wait any longer; get started right now.

You've come a long way already. Let's do a quick recap of what we have covered, using the TL;DRs from each chapter.

1. Adulting is hard, especially when it comes to money management. With some sass and a little smartass, I'm here to make the journey to financial freedom easy and fun. After reading this book and learning

the 7 Simple Steps, you'll finally have an easy-to-implement strategy that will help you gain control of your finances right away.

2. There is no hard and fast savings percentage rule because each situation is different. You must save a significant portion of your income. 10% won't get you anywhere. Up your savings game by increasing your income or decreasing your expenses.

3. Open a high-yield savings account to take advantage of compound interest and grow your money. Separate your savings into four buckets depending on how soon you will need the money. Bucket #1 is for emergencies, Bucket #2 is for big-ticket items within the next year, Bucket #3 is for big-ticket items more than a year away, and Bucket #4 is for retirement. Fill up Bucket #1 first, then work on Bucket #2 and #3 while contributing regularly to Bucket #4.

4. There's no such thing as good debt; it's either tolerable debt or bad debt. Compare your financing rate to the underlying asset's rate of appreciation to know for sure if you are making the right choice before going into debt.

5. You need good credit to buy big-ticket items and to qualify for lower insurance rates. The three main credit reporting agencies are TransUnion, Equifax, and Experian. The main factors that influence your credit score are payment history, debt utilization,

length of credit history, number of inquiries, and number and type of credit accounts.

6. Considering going to college? The cost of college these days is a significant financial burden and may not be financially viable. Recently graduated? Student loan payments can be consolidated at a lower interest rate to save you money. Saving for your child's education? Parents can take advantage of the tax benefits of a 529 plan.

7. Only use a credit card if you pay the balance in full, every month. Otherwise, you will end up paying hundreds of dollars in interest charges. If used wisely, credit cards offer fantastic benefits and rewards.

8. Other types of debt include home equity loans, personal loans, business loans, payday loans, and most commonly, mortgages. Interest rates and term lengths have the biggest impact on the total cost of your mortgage.

9. Stocks > Bonds.

10. Mutual funds are pools of multiple stocks chosen by a professional. Index funds are pools of multiple stocks that automatically track to a market index. Index funds > mutual funds > individual stocks.

11. Sell when the market is high and buy when the market is low. Only invest for the long term. Don't micromanage your investments.

12. My preferred strategy is to invest 25% of my account in each of the following: domestic small cap, domestic mid cap, domestic large cap, and international. Only invest in funds with less than 0.2% expense ratios.

13. Open an account with a discount broker to save on fees. To make a trade, you'll need the ticker symbol, quantity of shares, and order type.

14. The two most common types of retirement accounts are the 401(K) and IRA. Either account can be set up as traditional or Roth, and you will decide which type based on your current vs. future expected earnings. Think of retirement as the moment at which your passive income exceeds your expenses.

15. Your taxable income minus deductions equals your adjusted gross income (AGI.) Use your tax brackets and your AGI to determine your gross tax liability. Subtract tax credits to get your final tax liability. Compare this amount with how much you withheld the previous year to see if you'll get a refund or if you'll owe. If your refund is large, consider adjusting your withholdings so you do not continue to loan your money to the government interest-free.

16. If you have no dependents, you do not need life insurance. If people are dependent on you financially, then term life insurance is better than whole. Long-term disability insurance is sometimes more important than life insurance.

Now that you have the knowledge, we are going to piece together a strategy that is customized for your situation. There are some easy tasks throughout this book, like creating a budget. Then there are some more challenging ones, like figuring out how much of your Golden Number (remember, your extra money left over after expenses each month) should be allocated to debt payoff vs. savings vs. investing. I've boiled it down to 7 Simple Steps so that you can get started today and be well on your way to financial freedom.

Step One: Know Your Current Story

To move forward, you must know where you stand today. You'll need to compile ALL of your financial details. Go through the list below and write down dollar figures for each item. Want me to make your life easier for this step? Go to http://eepurl.com/c1ro7H to download my free excel worksheets that make compiling this information much more convenient. A gift from me to you.

- <u>Monthly spending</u>. You should already have all of your monthly expenses written down from the budgeting exercise.

- <u>Current after-tax income</u>. Write down all sources of your household income. Include income from any side gigs, alimony, or child support. Only count after-tax income (your take-home pay.)

- <u>Golden number</u>. Subtract your monthly expenses from your monthly income.

- <u>Total assets</u>. Assets are items that add to your net worth. This includes cash, money in checking or savings accounts, retirement accounts, investment accounts, the value of your home (not the amount of your mortgage), the value of your car, money that is owed to you, the value of any business that you own, and so forth. Write down a dollar figure for each item and then add them together to get the total.

- <u>Total liabilities</u>. Liabilities are items that deduct from your net worth. This includes loans, student debt, credit card debt, your mortgage, your car loan, and any other money that you owe to someone else. Write down a dollar figure for each item and then add them together to get the total.

- <u>Net worth</u>. Subtract your liabilities from your assets.

- <u>Debt details</u>. Write down every single loan, credit card, or debt that you have. Write down the balance and interest rate for each.

- <u>Retirement account</u>. Write down the balance and any details regarding an employer match.

Step Two: Brainstorm Your Financial Goals

You know where you are. Now, let's figure out where you
want to go. The next step is to brainstorm all of your
financial goals. Start with your savings goals and think
about your Buckets. One goal would be to fill up Bucket #1
with $1,000. Another would be to have at least 4.5 months'
worth of living expenses saved in Bucket #2, or the total
amount of money you'll need for big-ticket purchase within
the next year; whichever is greater. Bucket #3 is for
purchases more than a year away, and Bucket #4 is for
retirement. You should have a dollar amount in Buckets #1,
#2, and #3, and you should be contributing money from
every paycheck to Bucket #4.

Think about other financial goals you might have and write
those down too: paying off your student loans, paying off
your credit card debt, supporting someone financially, and
so forth.

Step Three: Grow Your Golden Number

Your Golden Number represents the amount of money you
have to work with each month. This amount is what you
will allocate to each of your buckets. I'm going to be straight
up with you: I can't get you far if you are only saving $100
per month. At that rate, it would take you ten months to fill
up Bucket #1. Ain't nobody got time for that. Refer back to
Chapter Two for ways to increase your income or decrease
your expenses. Even if your Golden Number is $1,000, you
should be focusing on ways to make your Golden Number

larger. Depending on your circumstances, even $2,000 might not be enough to hit your goals quickly.

For Step Three, brainstorm and implement at least five ways to grow your Golden Number.

In general, you'll channel your Golden Number towards one goal at a time. You won't divide your GN by six and make six equal payments to all six of your goals. Your Focus Goal will be what you focus on above all else; it will be your immediate, apply-as-much-money-towards, punch-it-in-the-face goal. The others will take a back seat. For example, if your Focus Goal is to pay off your Banana Republic credit card, you'll make minimum payments on all other debts and to your retirement account, and then put the vast majority of your GN towards Banana.

Step Four: Fill Up Bucket #1

Your first Focus Goal is Bucket #1. Don't even start contributing to your retirement yet. There's no use trying to do anything else until you have at least $1,000 in emergency savings.

So again, you'll make all of your minimum debt payments, because you have no choice, but *the rest of your Golden Number* goes towards Bucket #1 until it's filled up with $1,000. If you are doing this the right way, that is, being aggressive and working on growing your Golden Number, then this should only take you one to three months. If you feel like your progress is way too slow, increase your income or decrease your expenses even further. Surely you can make a dramatic effort for a couple months!

> *Remember, Bucket #1 is used for unforeseen and urgent emergencies only. If you ever need to use Bucket #1, immediately pause your Focus Goal and switch it back to Bucket #1. You should refill Bucket #1 ASAP if you ever use from or deplete it.*

Step Five: Determine Your Minimum Contribution to Bucket #4

From now on, you will always do one thing: contribute regularly to your retirement account. No ifs, ands, or buts. Think of it as a debt payment; you *must* make the minimum payment each month. We're going to set the minimum payment with Step Five.

If you have a 401(K), your employer might offer a matching contribution. First you need to find out what the contribution is and how it works. For example, if your employer offers a 100% matching contribution on your first 3%, then you better bet you're a$$ that you'll be contributing at least 3% of every paycheck. If they offer a 50% matching contribution on up to your first 6%, then you'll be putting in, at minimum, 6% on the reg. It's free money, so you want to make sure you get every cent of it! Determine how your employer match works and calculate how much per paycheck or month you need to contribute to maximize it.

"Uh, dude, to meet my full employer match, I would need to put my entire Golden Number in there." Uh, dude, then you need to increase your Golden Number. If at any point during the following exercises, your Golden Number is not enough to go around, you have one viable option: make your Golden Number larger. Or continue to live in the anxiety-inducing world of living paycheck to paycheck and swimming in debt. It's your choice.

If you don't have an employer match, then you have more flexibility on your minimum monthly payment to Bucket #4. You can set your minimum retirement contribution at $80 per month, for example, and you can always adjust (read: increase) it later.

Step Six: Prioritize and Achieve Your Goals

Now that Bucket #1 is filled up and your minimum retirement contribution is set, you can tackle the rest of your savings and debt goals. The only question is: which do you pick as your next Focus Goal?

You want to maximize the power of your money. You want to focus on the highest-interest rate things in your life, whether they are good or bad. Think back to some of the interest-rate comparisons we did when we were talking about how and when to go into debt for a purchase. Remember, you wouldn't use a 20%-interest-rate credit card to buy a painting that appreciates at a rate of 3%, because that would be dumb.

Whether you're paying off a high-interest debt or contributing to a high-yield investment, you'll want to tackle those high rates first. Let's say you have $1,000. You can either put it towards an investment that has a guaranteed 20% return or you can pay off your 1% interest-rate loan. What should you do? If you invest it, you'll gain $200, and you'll also pay $10 in interest from having the loan for another year. So you net +$190. But if you pay off the loan, you won't have to pay the interest, but you also won't gain $200, so you break even. Forgoing $200 to save yourself $10 is not something I'd high-five you for. Do you see how you can play the interest rates off each other to result in a net gain? That's why it's important to always tackle the highest-interest rate items first, whether it's a good guy or a bad guy.

Next exercise: list your interest rates in order from largest to smallest. For this exercise, do not include your mortgage if you have one.

You may be wondering why we are excluding your mortgage. Generally, out of all your debt, your mortgage is the only tolerable debt, since your house usually appreciates in value, and you are also building up equity over time. In the grand scheme of things, paying off your mortgage should be your last goal.

You should have already written down your debt details in Step One. Add your buckets to this list. Bucket #1 is already filled up at this point so don't include that. Bucket #2 will be invested in a high-yield savings account for around 1%. Buckets #3 and #4 will be invested in the stock market, where it's impossible to predict your return. You might lose money; you might gain money. For our purposes, let's assume an average of a 6% return. Please read my disclaimer at the end of the book to remind yourself that I personally cannot guarantee stock market returns.

Your list should look something like this, listed in order of highest interest rate to lowest interest rate:

Debt	Balance	Interest Rate
Ann Taylor Credit Card	$250	23.5%
CapitalOne Credit Card	$5,100	22.5%
Discover It Credit Card	$378	20.0%
Home Equity Loan	$10,050	10.2%
Bucket #4	LOTS	6.0%
Bucket #3	$30,000	6.0%
Fannie Mae student loan	$12,890	5.5%
Bucket #2	$7,000	1.0%

Logically, your Focus Goal should be the highest-interest-rate item on your list. Let's do an example. Let's say Stephanie's situation is identical to that in the table above. She has a few credit cards, a home equity loan, a student loan, and her buckets.

Stephanie works as a lab researcher at a company that offers a 401(K) plan with no employer contribution. She's decided that her minimum retirement contribution to her IRA is $50 per month. Stephanie's monthly after-tax income is $2,250, and her monthly expenses are $1,780. That means her Golden Number is $470.

The highest-interest-rate item is an Ann Taylor Credit Card, so that should be Stephanie's focus goal. She'll get the most bang for her buck by paying off that debt and discontinuing that exorbitant interest rate. She should make her $50 per month minimum contribution to Bucket #4 for retirement (because remember, you *always* make that minimum contribution, no matter what) and allocate the rest of her Golden Number, or $420, to the Ann Taylor card. The good news is, with the low balance, she'll pay that off immediately.

Once she crosses the Ann Taylor card off, Stephanie should move to the next-highest-interest-rate item: her CapitalOne credit card. And so on and so forth.

For every rule, there is an exception. I wouldn't recommend ignoring Bucket #2 in Stephanie's scenario, even for interest-rate purposes. That's because if she suddenly lost her job, Bucket #1 won't keep her afloat for enough time to find a new job, unless she's really lucky. Bucket #2 is important as a backup emergency savings. Another option, in the scenario above, is to continue making the $50 contributions to Bucket #4, contribute another $50 or so to Bucket #2, and THEN put the rest of the Golden Number towards the Focus Goal.

Some of you will disagree with that because logically it doesn't make sense: you should tackle your highest-interest-rate item before anything else. That's true; after all, the credit card costs way more in interest than savings would earn. It's up to you and what you're most comfortable with. If you're debt-averse, by all means focus on that card. If you'd rather save while paying down debt, then contribute a little to Bucket #2 each month too. I personally would pay off all debt before saving anything over and above what's already in Bucket #1.

I'd like to clarify another nuance. Let's use Victoria the veterinarian as an example. Her list looks like this:

Debt	Balance	Interest Rate
Bucket #4	LOTS	6.0%
Bucket #3	$45,000	6.0%
Fannie Mae student loan	$5,350	5.5%
Bucket #2	$11,000	1.0%

Victoria's only debt is a student loan with 5.5% interest. Bucket #1 is filled up, so she is working on Bucket #2 and then Bucket #3. To maximize her employer match, she is contributing $300/month to her retirement account in Bucket #4 with a 6% return.

Technically, the order to tackle these three goals based on the interest rates would be: 1) Retirement account at 6%, 2) Bucket #3 at 6%, 3) Student loan at 5.5%, and 4) Bucket #2 at 1%.

But Victoria's retirement account is bottomless. She'll never "fill" it up. If she focuses on that goal, she won't ever meet it, and she'd be ignoring the student loan debt. And Bucket #2 is important too! In a scenario like Victoria's, I'd recommend contributing that $300/month to the retirement account, putting a little towards Bucket #2, and putting MOST of her Golden Number to the student loan debt. Getting that last bit of debt paid off will feel great!

As you achieve a goal, you'll swap it out with the next goal. Get that credit card paid off? Swap in the next-highest-interest-rate debt. Get Bucket #2 filled up? Move on to Bucket #3. By the end of all this, you'll have Buckets #1 through #3 filled up and no debt! Can you imagine how incredible that will be? At that point, you have a choice of either maxing out your retirement contribution, saving more in Buckets #2 or #3 for the heck of it, or *gasp* spending more. You heard me!

Step Seven: Complete an Annual Review

Each year you'll want to sit down and go through this process again. Write down your current financials and goals. Think of new ways to grow your Golden Number. Re-evaluate your monthly contribution to Bucket #4. Make sure Bucket #1 is still full. Re-prioritize the rest of your goals.

Keep your records from each review. Completing an annual review will help you reset and refocus. If you are making fast progress on the 7 Steps, do a review every six months; there's nothing like a little self-validation!

I also recommend updating your balance sheet every month. If you're following the steps, seeing your net worth grow will be a huge motivator for you. It's exciting to see how much progress you've made in only a few months.

The Money Honey Plan In Action

TL;DR See how the 7 Steps work from beginning to end.

Congrats, my dear friend! You're at the finish line. I want to run you through an entire scenario to help you tie everything together. Consider yourself friends a bada$$ named Amber.

As a team, you and I are going to help out Amber. Amber is a 27-year-old cybersecurity architect living in Massachusetts. Although she was only making $34,000 right out of college, she recently landed a higher-paying gig at a global firm making $60,000. Snaps for Amber.

Because of her student loan debt and high cost of living, Amber struggled financially for a few years after graduation. She resorted to opening a couple credit cards to make ends meet for a while.

Although she has $4,100 in an IRA, the only other savings she has is the $500 sign-on bonus that she received from her new employer a few months ago when she started. Her new employer provides health insurance and offers a 100% match on the first 3% that Amber contributes to her 401(K).

Amber has a boyfriend, Zachary, and a simultaneously ugly and adorable pug named Belle. She lives with Zachary in a small two-bedroom, one-bathroom apartment that they rent for $1,500 per month. Amber splits the rent and utilities 50/50 with Zachary.

Amber is desperate to get out of debt, and she feels she has no excuses now that she's making more money. She has a total of $47,000 left in student loan debt with an interest rate of 5%. She has another $12,000 in credit card debt with an interest rate of 20%. She also has a car loan of $5,000 at a 3% interest rate. Yikes, Amber needs us!

Amber's monthly after-tax income is $3,500. She uses Mint to track her monthly expenses, so she knows that the following is accurate:

Type	Monthly Amount
Half of rent	$750
Half of utilities (Water, Cable, Wi-fi, Gas, Electric)	$160
Renters Insurance	$19
Minimum Car Payment	$180
Car Insurance	$80
Car Maintenance	$40
Gas	$130
Minimum Credit Card Payment	$137
Minimum Student Loan Payment	$188
Phone Bill	$42
Pet Care	$105
Gym Membership	$39
Groceries & Eating Out	$580
Gifts (Christmas, birthdays)	$70
Shopping	$200
Personal Grooming	$130
Entertainment	$70
Subscriptions (Netflix, Amazon Prime, Costco)	$20
Charitable Donations	$20
Other/Misc.	$150
TOTAL	$3,110

With a monthly income of $3,500 and monthly expenses of
$3,110, Amber's Golden Number is $390. Red flag anyone?
She could be doing a lot better.

Let's take a look at her net worth. If you haven't caught on,
we are currently compiling all of Amber's financial
information for Step One.

Type	Amount
ASSETS:	
IRA	$4,100
Cash & Checking account	$126
Savings	$500
Value of car	$10,000
TOTAL ASSETS	$14,726
LIABILITIES:	
Student loan	$47,000
Credit card	$12,000
Car loan	$5,000
TOTAL LIABILITIES	$64,000
NET WORTH	($49,274)

Amber's assets are $14,726 and her liabilities are $64,000.
Her net worth is negative $49,274... awkward. She has a lot
of work to do to turn that around, but at least she knows
where she stands.

Step Two is for Amber to brainstorm her financial goals. She starts by filling in her savings buckets and comes up with the following goals:

Bucket #2 needs to have at least three to six months' worth of living expenses. Using her current expenses, 4.5 months-worth is almost $14,000. Amber's only savings goals for the next year are travel-related. She would need $2,250 to enjoy a trip to Mexico with Zachary and also to fly home for Christmas. Out of these two numbers, her living expenses are greater, so that's what she writes for Bucket #2.

In a few years, Amber wants to buy herself a new car, and she eventually wants to buy a house and get married. She's estimating that those three things will cost $90,000, so that's her amount for Bucket #3.

Amber's other goals are to save for retirement and pay down all of her debt.

Amber can now move onto Step Three and think of ways to grow her Golden Number. She brainstorms ideas for increasing her income first. After talking it over with Zachary, they decide to list their second bedroom for rent on AirBNB. Amber thinks this will bring in another $400 per month (of which she will take $200.) Amber also decides to tutor some local college students two evenings a week. If she tutors for $40 per hour, for two hours per week, she will make another $320. Incorporating these two ideas will increase her monthly after-tax income by $364, from $3,500 to $3,864. She's happy with this and can always incorporate more ideas later.

Next, Amber looks at her expenses. Looking at her list, she sees some obvious places she can cut down. One of her largest expenses is $580 per month for groceries and eating out. She reflects on all the happy hours she's attended lately and the nights that she and Zachary go out for dinner and drinks. This one is easy: Amber vows to cook more, eat out less, and consume less alcohol. She is positive she can get this expense down to $400 per month.

Amber looks through the list again and only focuses on the discretionary expenses. Her fixed expenses like rent and debt payments cannot be lowered, but some discretionary expenses such as highlights, manicures, and pedicures, can be given up. On some of her bills, she calls and asks for a discount or threatens to switch to a new provider. She wins a lower monthly bill on her car insurance and cell phone. She finds a cheaper grooming and day-care place for Belle and finds a cheaper, closer gym membership. She also unplugs electrical items that aren't in use, turns off lights more often, and takes shorter showers. She knows that every dollar makes a difference. After attempting to lower the amount in every category, Amber's revised budget looks like this:

Type	Monthly Amount
Half of rent	$750
Half of utilities (Water, Cable, Wifi, Gas, Electric)	~~$160~~ $155
Renters Insurance	$19
Minimum Car Payment	$180
Car Insurance	~~$80~~ $70
Car Maintenance	$40
Gas	$130
Minimum Credit Card Payment	$137
Minimum Student Loan Payment	$188
Phone Bill	~~$42~~ $38

Pet Care	~~$105~~ $75
Gym Membership	~~$39~~ $30
Groceries & Eating Out	~~$580~~ $400
Gifts (Christmas, birthdays)	~~$70~~ $50
Shopping	~~$200~~ $30
Personal Grooming	~~$130~~ $60
Entertainment	~~$70~~ $30
Subscriptions (Netflix, Amazon Prime, Costco)	$20
Charitable Donations	$20
Other/Misc	$150
TOTAL	$2,572

Now, Amber is realizing this is doable. With some sacrifice and a few tricks, she knows she can stick to her new budget, which is $538 less than her old one! Plus, she can update Bucket #2 with this lesser spending amount. Instead of needing $14,000 to survive for 4.5 months were she to lose her job, she only needs $11,574. She writes the new number in Bucket #2.

Don't forget that Amber will be bringing in more money each month. With her lower expenses and increase in income, her new Golden Number is $1,292! Her GN increased by $902. She never dreamed she could save that much every month. Seeing that number gets her pumped up to continue onto Step Number Four.

Amber is thrilled because it will take her less than one month to fill up Bucket #1. She already has $500 saved, so with her next paycheck she puts $500 more into Bucket #1.

Onto Step Five! Amber's new employer matches 100% of the first 3% that Amber contributes to her 401(K). She calculates that she will need to contribute $150 per month to take full advantage of the matching contribution. So out of her $1,292 Golden Number, $150 will go towards Bucket #4, forever and always (until she increases it.)

Now Amber is on Step Six: prioritizing the rest of her goals. She lists out her debts and savings buckets in order of highest interest rate to lowest:

Debt	Balance	Interest Rate
Credit Card	$12,000	20.0%
Bucket #4	LOTS	6%
Bucket #3	$90,000	6%
Student Loan	$47,000	5.0%
Car Loan	$5,000	3.0%
Bucket #2	$11,574	1.0%

Amber knows that the smartest thing to do is to continue putting $150 into Bucket #4 and allocate all the rest of her Golden Number to her credit card debt since the interest rate is so high. However, she wants to fill up Bucket #2 as well. She decides to put $150 per month into Bucket #4, $125 per month into Bucket #2, and the rest ($1,017) towards her credit card. That way, she knows she will have her credit card debt entirely paid off within the next year! Amber is blown away by everything she can achieve by putting a budget into place and following the 7 Steps.

Amber realizes that by only saving $125 per month in Bucket #2, she won't be able to do both her Mexico trip and her Christmas trip home. After one year she will only have $1500 in Bucket #2, so she'll need to pick between the two. She is willing to postpone her Mexico trip for another year in the name of kicking her finances in the a$$.

One year later...

One year later, how do you think Amber is doing? Let's take a look.

Amber has successfully paid off her $12,000 in credit card debt. She had a slight setback about four months in when she had to dip into her Emergency Savings and use $400 for an urgent car expense. The next month, she immediately filled Bucket #1 back up. Despite the minor setback, she was still able to pay off her credit card debt within one year because she continued to find ways to grow her Golden Number. She's now tutoring three evenings per week, and she's cut her expenses even further. She's thrilled by the milestone and encouraged to keep going.

Here's how Amber's balance sheet and net worth look now:

Type	Amount
ASSETS:	
IRA	~~$4100~~ $4,346
401(K)	$1,995
Cash & Checking account	~~$126~~ $175
Bucket #1	~~$500~~ $1,000
Bucket #2	$750
Resell value of car	~~$10,000~~ $9,000
TOTAL ASSETS	~~$14,726~~ $17,266
LIABILITIES:	
Student loan	~~$47,000~~ $46,500
Credit card	~~$12,000~~ 0
Car loan	~~$5,000~~ $4,500
TOTAL LIABILITIES	~~$64,000~~ $51,000
NET WORTH	~~($49,274)~~ ($33,734)

Wow! Amber increased her net worth by over $15,000 in one year! Keep in mind that her IRA was invested in the stock market and appreciated in value in the past year. Amber saved $1,500 in Bucket #2 but spent $750 to fly home for Christmas. The value of her car decreased by $1,000. On the liability side, her credit card debt is gone, and she has continued making minimum payments on the student loan debt and car loan, so those decreased slightly. All in all, her wealth grew by $15,540 over the past year. Snaps for Amber.

Time for Step Seven, the annual review. Amber's after-tax monthly income is now $3,976 (because of her one extra tutoring session per week), and her current monthly expenses are $2,403, meaning her Golden Number is larger than ever at $1,573. Imagine having $1,500 extra dollars each month! You'd be able to pay down debt and save money so quickly.

Now that Amber has achieved her first goal, she wants to rethink her strategy going forward. Here's what her list of interest rates looks like:

Debt	Balance	Interest Rate
~~Credit Card~~	~~$12,000~~	~~20.0%~~
Bucket #4	N/A	6%
Bucket #3	$90,000	6%
Student Loan	$46,500	5.0%
Car Loan	$4,500	3.0%
Bucket #2	$10,814	1.0%

Next in line regarding interest rates are Buckets #4 and #3. But Amber knows that Bucket #4 is an ongoing goal, and Bucket #2 needs to be filled up before Bucket #3. Amber will not focus on Bucket #3 at all right now, and she will continue to make the $150 per month contribution to her 401(K). So, next in line is her student loan; she is ready to attack that sucker with a vengeance. She also wants to contribute even more to Bucket #2 this year. Of her $1,573 Golden Number, she puts $150 per month towards Bucket

#4, $250 per month towards Bucket #2, and the remaining $1,173 per month towards her student loans. Amber thinks that if she sets her mind to it, she can get her student loans paid off within three years.

At this point, Amber is confident of her strategy moving forward. She will continue to grow her Golden Number, save for Bucket #2 and Bucket #4, and pay down her student loans. She thinks back to when she was making $32,000 and was up to her eyeballs in debt, living paycheck-to-paycheck. Now she has $1,500 in extra cash every month, and she's made significant progress paying down her debt. She dreams of the day when her debt is paid off, her buckets are full, and she has $1,500 extra in play money each month! Envisioning that moment motivates Amber to keep aggressively improving her financial situation.

Spoiler alert: this could be you.

Get Started Now—What to Expect

TL;DR The first three steps can be completed in one afternoon, so get started now. Expect roadblocks and don't get discouraged. Set yourself up for success by writing down and publicizing your goals, setting expectations with family and friends, and finding an accountability buddy. No excuses. You can do this!

So, how are you feeling?

A. Nervous

B. Overwhelmed

C.   Excited

D.   All of the above

Most of you will say D. That's normal. Reaching your goals
might take years, and something that takes years tends to
sound like an impossible undertaking. But not if you focus
on completing one step at a time. Let's review the 7 Steps
and how long each one will take.

Step One	Know Your Current Story	1 hour
Step Two	Brainstorm Your Financial Goals	20 min
Step Three	Grow Your Golden Number	45 min brainstorm
Step Four	Fill Up Bucket #1	1-3 months
Step Five	Determine Your Minimum Contribution to Bucket #4	10 min
Step Six	Prioritize & Achieve Your Goals	Depends
Step Seven	Complete an Annual Review	2 hours per year

You can knock out Step One and Step Two in an hour and
twenty minutes. You can brainstorm for Step Three in

another 45 minutes. The first three steps are easy and quick! You could have them completed in one evening or one weekend afternoon.

Remember how excited Amber felt after she completed the first three steps and realized how much more she could be saving each month on her new budget? That's how you'll feel too! Within a few hours you can map out your entire strategy to achieve complete financial freedom. Then you have to stick to it. Once you begin making progress, you'll be motivated to keep going and to be even more aggressive à la Amber. The hardest part of going on a run is always taking the first step.

Warning: expect roadblocks. You will inevitably get discouraged along the way. Maybe you'll dip into Bucket #1 for an emergency right after you filled up Bucket #1. That's what Bucket #1 is for, silly! That's no reason to get discouraged. Be excited for having a system that works, and for having the money in Bucket #1 to use in the first place instead of putting another $500 on your credit card.

Or you might accidentally-but-not-really splurge and go over budget in one category. In this case, you might feel guilt-ridden and $hitty about yourself because you had one job. You know what? Give yourself a break. It takes time to become a financial wizard. By no means should you give yourself a "free pass," but understand that adjustments are needed. Don't be too hard on yourself. Recommit and refocus the next month.

At some point, you will go from feeling discouraged to feeling deprived. Denying yourself of things that you want and are used to having is challenging. After a few months of foregoing your fave Starbucks drink for homemade coffee instead, you'll be craving the SB. Keep pushing on. Adjust your budget by lowering it elsewhere if you want to work something back into your lifestyle. You can do this. You are strong. You are strong enough to delay instant gratification for something much more important: your financial freedom.

You will sometimes feel left out. Wanna know what happens when you cut back on entertainment or alcohol expenses? You don't get to go out with your friends as much. There's no way around this. It's a sacrifice. There are plenty of other ways to have fun (and even get a little tipsy) without spending $10 a pop at the local bar. Pre-game at your house, volunteer to be designated driver more often, and limit how often you go out. Instead of getting brunch every weekend, take turns with your friends making breakfast and then finding something fun to do outside. Broaden your horizons!

Keys to Success

To guarantee your success, you should implement the following suggestions. First and foremost, <u>write down your goals</u>. Write down the benefits of completing said goals. What will paying off debt enable you to do? How will Bucket #2 impact your life? What is motivating you to do this? Why are you sick and tired of living the way you are?

What do you want to feel like when you think about your finances?

Take your time to consider these questions so you can uncover your "Why." Your Why will be unique to you and your situation. My Why is largely driven by my fear of being financially dependent on someone. Maybe your Why is that you want to have the power of being able to financially help out a family member or friend in need. Maybe your Why is that your number one dream is to be able to travel the world, and that requires money and financial freedom. Think of your Why. Write it in large letters on your mirror, on your car dashboard, on your front door, on your refrigerator. Look at it every day. Allow it to instill purpose and determination.

Share your goal. Research shows that sharing your goal with others adds an accountability factor and makes you more likely to succeed in achieving your goal.[14] You don't have to tell the world that you have $30,000 in credit card debt, but you should be concrete. Maybe your goal is to pay off all of your credit card debt within the next year. Perfect; make it known.

Sharing your goal with your support system will result in two benefits: 1) Your friends and family will encourage you and share in your success with every milestone, and 2) You set expectations for how your lifestyle might change in the coming months and years. Cutting back on expenses *will* have an impact on your social life. When I'm "splurging," it's because I'm meeting friends for dinner and drinks.

When I'm "cutting back," I find other things to do with friends, like go on a walk in the park. Set expectations for what will change in your life so your support network can adjust accordingly.

A short email to friends and family such as the following will help set expectations: *"Friends and family, I'd like to share with you an important goal I have this year. I'm committing to paying off 100% of my credit card debt within the next 12 months. I'm super excited about this goal because (fill in the blank.) I know this will be tough which is why I wanted to share it with you and garner your support and enthusiasm. Achieving this goal will require me to (insert how this could impact your life and your interactions with them). I'll keep you all updated as I make progress! Thanks for always being there for me!"* If you're not comfortable emailing this, you can always call or text each individual family member or friend. I guarantee that this simple but powerful message will be received with excitement and support, and you will be able to feed off that to stay motivated and focused.

<u>Keep emphasizing your goals.</u> Inevitably, the people around you will invite you to spend money with them because they forget what you are trying to achieve. Giving them a friendly verbal reminder and an alternative plan works fine. When your co-worker asks you go to out for lunch and it's not in your budget, don't be afraid to say, "Oh remember, I'm cutting back on eating out but, if you want to grab your own takeout, I'd be happy to eat with you in the breakroom!" After enough reinforcement, your lifestyle will

eventually sink into their brain, and they will begin proactively inviting you to things that they know will work for you.

For example, one weekend when I was eating healthy, my college friend invited me to come visit her for a day. Knowing I was on a diet, she suggested we get ingredients to make salads and take our dogs to a nearby park to get some exercise. We had so much fun that day, and I was able to stick to my goals!

Find an accountability buddy. Sharing your goal publicly increases your feelings of accountability, and finding a specific person will enforce that even more. This person should be close enough to you that they'll give you some tough love every now and then. This person should be working towards a concrete goal for themselves. It's best if their goal is also money-related, but that's not a requirement.

Have someone in mind? Approach this person and propose that you check in with each other weekly. The purpose of these weekly check-ins is to share what goals you achieved this week, while also venting and problem-solving on what's challenging you and what should be adjusted. Getting some outside perspective as you begin your journey will add tremendous value. Think of someone who would be a great accountability buddy and call them right now.

Reward yourself on occasion for progress made. Find small, inexpensive ways to treat yourself: some flowers from Trader Joe's, a new novel you've been eyeing from Half

Price Books, those gourmet chocolates you love, your favorite bottle of wine, or a walk in the park with your dog or kid. Don't treat yourself every *day*. Reserve it for when you are feeling discouraged and want to acknowledge your hard work or when you've crossed another financial goal off your list.

Get Started... Now!

Don't wait a second longer. Your journey to financial freedom starts today. Start right now with Step One, even if you only have fifteen minutes. In those few minutes, I promise that you will already feel a sense of relief by taking action. Then, look at your schedule and plan when you will complete Steps Two and Three within the next couple days.

No excuses. Nothing is more important right now then looking out for your own financial future and taking care of yourself. Don't be the person that says, "I'll wait until this weekend so I can do the first Three Steps all at once." No. Start now. If you don't, you might find ten other excuses by then for why you should continue to put it off.

Step One is easy; you are compiling information. Grab your laptop, snuggle up on the couch, and log in to your accounts. Like I said, the hardest part of going on a run is the first step out the door. If you can push yourself to get started right now, your odds of succeeding quadruple. Before you know it, a year will have passed, and you will have achieved several financial milestones.

If you'd like, email me every step of the way at moneyhoneyrachel@gmail.com. I want to hear about how YOU, my beautiful reader, are doing. If you've stayed with me this far, I consider you a close friend, and I shall share in your setbacks and your achievements. I believe in you, but YOU have to believe in you. Now get out there, kick some a$$, and get rich!

Dear Rachel Advice Column

Dear Rachel,

I'm 33, and I feel way behind in terms of saving for my financial future. I have a little credit card debt. Is it better to save for my 401(K) while slowly paying off the debt, or get the debt down THEN save for retirement? I have consolidated all my credit card debt to a 0% interest card for the next two years.

Dear Getting-My-Priorities-Straight,

There's no need to make this an either-or situation, because paying down debt and saving for retirement are both important. First, does your employer make a matching contribution on your 401(K)? If so, I would put enough into your 401(K) to take advantage of the full match since that's free money. The rest should go to the credit card debt until it's paid off. If your employer does *not* offer any matching contribution, then let's take a look at the CC debt first. Your 0% interest on your debt buys you time to pay off the CC debt without racking up even more in interest charges. I would take advantage of the entire two years for which you have 0% interest. Set up a plan for yourself that ensures the CC is paid off in exactly two years. Apply any extra amount per month to the 401(K). Again, don't pick one goal over the other. Incorporate one of these strategies so that you are tackling both simultaneously.

Dear Rachel,

What's the best piece of financial advice you've ever received?

Dear Curious George,

I love this question so much that I polled friends, family, and some other financial whizzes for their responses. Here's what we came up with:

- Don't buy things you can't afford. If you can't pay cash for it, you can't afford it.

- Give every dollar in your bank account a job.

- Don't use credit cards as gift cards. When you get your first CC, you might think, "4K limit!? I'm rich!" …You are not rich.

- Automatic deposits from your paycheck make saving so much easier.

- Max out the employer match to your 401(K).

- Live below your means.

- Pay yourself first. As in, save first, spend what's left.

Dear Rachel,

I recently earned a bonus at work (yay!) and I'm trying to be responsible and put it towards debt. Is it best to put it towards paying off one card in particular or spread it over all three of my credit cards? Halp!

Dear Ms. Responsibility,

To get the most bang for your bonus, put it all towards the card that has the higher interest rate while paying minimums on the other two. This will reduce the amount of your monthly interest charges. Continue to put all extra money towards the highest interest rate card until it's paid off, then move to the next highest interest rate card. If they all have equal interest rates, pay off the smallest balance first. You will feel productive and motivated getting one paid off. Then you can focus on the others.

Dear Rachel,

Credit card debt. I'm lost and don't see any way out. It's time for me to take this more seriously but I don't know where to start. I make $45,000, I work a side hustle, and I'm going to *grad school. I am married with three kids. I try to pay my credit cards down, but then life happens. I have three cards and less than $6,000 in debt total, so it shouldn't be that hard, right? Why is it for me? What else can I do? I don't know what to change.*

Dear Lost & Discouraged,

What I'm hearing is that you've made progress in the past, but that something always interrupts your progress. That's why it's so important to get Bucket #1 filled up first. Remember, Bucket #1 is for emergency savings and should hold at least $1,000. So pause for a moment on the credit card debt. Make the minimum payments for now. Do everything in your power to increase your income or decrease your expenses so you can fill up Bucket #1. Create a list of all the things you do for fun that aren't truly necessary and decide where to cut back so you can put the extra amount into Bucket #1. While you are working on that, look into getting a debt consolidation loan from your bank (only if they offer a lower interest rate.) Bank rates are typically way better than the 25% the card is scamming you for. By consolidating, you'll only have one payment to tackle, and at a lower interest rate. Once you have the safety net of Bucket #1 in place, you'll be able to pay down your new, lower-interest-rate loan with no interruptions. And if "life happens," you have your emergency savings to fall back on, not your credit cards. Emergencies will become an inconvenience, not a catastrophe. You can do this.

Dear Rachel,

I will be making $98,000 a year from now and I want to buy a house at that point. How much house can I afford on that salary? I'm 26, single, and don't have any debt.

Dear Making Bank,

Technically you could afford a LOT of house on that salary... Probably more house than you'd ever need, depending on where you live. With a 6% interest rate, 30-year mortgage, and a 35% debt-to-income ratio, we are talking over $300,000 of house. If you're living in a more expensive city, $300,000 might get you a reasonable, modest house. If you're living in a city with a relatively lower cost-of-living, please forget that $300,000 number immediately because, as a young, single, working professional, living in a mansion is wholly unnecessary. So, let's reframe the question. Instead of how much can you afford, let's ask how much do you want to be paying each month? Think about what you're paying in rent right now and how much more you'd feel comfortable paying while still aggressively increasing your savings and retirement account. Maybe you're paying $800/month now, and you're okay with increasing that to $1,200/month. Using an online mortgage calculator, that payment amount translates to a $200,000 house. But don't forget to work in a budget for house maintenance, repairs, and renovations; houses break a lot and they're expensive. So in reality, $1200/month might get you a $150,000 house. The size and condition of a house will depend on your location, but please don't buy some luxurious house because you can. You're smarter than that.

The second part of the home buying equation is saving enough money for a down payment. Unless you qualify for an FHA or VA loan, you'll likely have to put the standard 20% down. 20% of $150,000 is $30,000. That's a pretty large sum, and you won't be buying a house without it. Focus your efforts on that for now so that in a year you're ready to buy. Good luck!

Dear Rachel,

I'm in desperate need of savings tips since I never learned how to save properly and am feeling the pressure. Can you lend some advice on savings tips and tricks for someone who doesn't know how?

Dear Savings-Illiterate,

Pay yourself first. Set up an automatic deposit from each paycheck into a savings account. That way it's forced and you won't even think about it. Also, there are all these fancy new savings apps these days like Acorn and Qapital. Download one and use it. Track your spending on Mint. Don't buy things because you can. After filling a shopping cart of clothes or shoes or groceries, ask yourself if you NEED those items. Find an accountability buddy and text her before every purchase. It will force you to re-evaluate that item. Put a Savings Jar in the kitchen and decorate it all cute, and then throw all your spare change in it at the end of each day. Saving more money takes a lot of willpower and determination, but you can do it!

Dear Rachel,

I've been kicking a$$ with my budget lately (woohoo!) and feeling way less stressed about money each month, but now I want to go out and buy all the things that I've been denying myself for so long! What are some little, inexpensive ways you treat yourself for a job well done?

Dear Deprived One,

A Milky Way Bar. Seriously. Those bitche$ are delicious.

Dear Rachel,

I have a decent amount left over after expenses each month, but I don't know how to juggle my student loans, savings accounts, and retirement accounts. I have various student loans with interest rates between 4% and 6%. I have $500/month to allocate for debt pay off and savings. What should I do?

Dear Dazed and Confused,

Start with Bucket #1 and make sure you have at least $1,000 in emergency savings. Do that before anything else. Then for Bucket #4, if your employer offers a matching contribution to your retirement account, put in enough to take advantage of the entire match. If not, put in something, even if it's only $50 per month. Now you have to choose how to allocate the rest of your Golden Number—let's say it's $450—between Bucket #2 and student loans. Since student loans have the higher interest rate, logically you should put all $450 towards the loans. However, it's okay to put a small portion into Bucket #2 to simultaneously build up more savings. After the student loans are paid off, focus on filling up Bucket #2 and then Bucket #3.

Dear Rachel,

When should I start saving for retirement?

Dear Procrastinator,

Now.

Dear Rachel,

I know you said to focus on the highest-interest-rate items first. For me right now that's Bucket #3 since I already have #1 and #2 filled up. However, I have a few student loans at a rate of 3% to 4% and another personal loan at a rate of 2%. I hate having this debt; it stresses me out! I'd much rather pay it off first, then fill up Bucket #3. Can I?

Dear Debt-Averse,

Yes. Let's talk about debt aversion. Some people like me are so debt-averse that they would move mountains to avoid it. They'd rather save money for three years to buy a car with cash instead of taking out a 0.5% interest loan. On the other hand, some people aren't emotionally burdened by the fact that they owe someone $3,000. Think about how you perceive debt. Do you think debt is evil and should be avoided at all costs? Or do you think debt is a normal part of life and not a big deal? Does having student loans or credit card debt stress you out? How much stress and why? Would you rather save up enough money to purchase a big-ticket item in full (think: car, engagement ring) or would you rather get a low-interest loan? Emotionally, does debt feel like a burden or something that weighs you down, or do you not give it much thought? Everyone was raised differently and had different learning experiences through life, so we all feel differently about debt. Understanding your relationship with debt will help you prioritize your goals. For instance, if I had credit card debt, knowing what a psychological toll that takes on me, I would make it a higher priority to pay it off. It sounds like you are pretty similar. If this is the case, it's not worth the stress to continue holding onto those debts if you'd rather pay them off. Go for it! Bucket #3 can wait.

Dear Rachel,

Why is financial adulting so hard?

Dear Struggle Bus,

Because we have no standard financial education system in place. So essentially we're all on our own to figure this $hit out. Hopefully, this book made it easier...

Acronyms

<u>AF</u>: As F***. For when something needs to be emphasized.

<u>AKA</u>: Also Known As.

<u>ASAP</u>: As Soon As Possible.

<u>BAE</u>: Before All Else. For when you love something or someone.

<u>BRB</u>: Be Right Back.

<u>BS</u>: Bull$hit.

<u>BTW</u>: By The Way.

<u>FOMO</u>: Fear Of Missing Out. For when you're scared of missing out on all the fun.

<u>FTW</u>: For The Win.

<u>FYI</u>: For Your Information.

<u>IMO</u>: In My Opinion.

<u>LOL</u>: Laugh Out Loud. For when something is funny.

<u>MF</u>: Motherf*****. For a$$holes. Or cool bitche$.

<u>MVP</u>: Most Valuable Player. For when something or someone is awesome.

<u>SMH</u>: Shaking My Head. The new eye-roll.

<u>SO</u>: Significant Other.

<u>TL;DR</u>: Too Long; Didn't Read. For giving the short version of the story.

<u>V</u>: Very. For when "very" is too hard to type out.

References

1. Dennis J. One in Three Americans Prepare a Detailed Household Budget. Gallup website. http://www.gallup.com/poll/162872/one-three-americans-prepare-detailed-household-budget.aspx. June 13, 2013. Accessed August 29, 2017.

2. Quentin F. Half of American families are living paycheck to paycheck. Marketwatch website. http://www.marketwatch.com/story/half-of-americans-are-desperately-living-paycheck-to-paycheck-2017-04-04. April 30, 2017. Accessed August 29, 2017.

3. Chris M. Average Savings Account Balance in the U.S.: A Statistical Breakdown. ValuePenguin website. https://www.valuepenguin.com/banking/average-savings-account-balance. June 2, 2017. Accessed August 29, 2017.

4. Elyssa K. 1 in 3 Americans Has Saved $0 for Retirement. Time website. http://time.com/money/4258451/retirement-savings-survey/. March 14, 2016. Accessed August 29, 2017.

5. Consumer Credit – G.19. Federal Reserve website. https://www.federalreserve.gov/releases/g19/curren

t/default.htm. August 7, 2017. Accessed August 29, 2017.

6. Education Center: Personal Finance Statistics. Debt website. https://www.debt.com/edu/personal-finance-statistics/. Accessed August 29, 2017.

7. Average Credit Score in America: 2017 Facts & Figures. ValuePenguin website. https://www.valuepenguin.com/average-credit-score. Accessed August 29, 2017.

8. Young Money Survey. TD Ameritrade website. http://www.amtd.com/newsroom/research-and-story-ideas/research-and-story-ideas-details/2017/Young-Money-Survey/default.aspx. May 11, 2017. Accessed August 29, 2017.

9. Jamie H. Understanding The Tax Benefits of 529 Plans. Forbes website. https://www.forbes.com/sites/jamiehopkins/2016/09/15/understanding-the-tax-benefits-of-529-plans/#7d4f3e6d19aa. September 15, 2016. Accessed August 29, 2017.

10. Great News: There's Another Recession Coming. Mr. Money Mustache website. http://www.mrmoneymustache.com/2017/06/20/next-recession/comment-page-2/. June 20, 2017. Accessed September 4, 2017.

11. Jonnelle M. Do any mutual funds ever beat the market? Hardly. The Washington Post website. https://www.washingtonpost.com/news/get-

there/wp/2015/03/17/do-any-mutual-funds-ever-beat-the-market-hardly/?utm_term=.656dd04822ff. March 17, 2015. Accessed August 29, 2017.

12. Chip C. Should You Invest for the Long-Term or Cash Out Quick? Equities website. https://www.equities.com/news/buy-hold-or-not. April 6, 2017. Accessed August 29, 2017.

13. Ellen C. You'll Need $2 Million Before You Can Think of Retirement. The Street Website. https://www.thestreet.com/story/13465544/1/you-ll-need-2-million-before-you-can-think-of-retirement.html. February 20, 2016. Accessed August 29, 2017.

14. Jason R. Look at how many pages are in the federal tax code. Washington Examiner website. http://www.washingtonexaminer.com/look-at-how-many-pages-are-in-the-federal-tax-code/article/2563032. April 15, 2016. Accessed August 29, 2017.

15. Matt W. Today is Tax Day. Facebook. https://www.facebook.com/MattWalshBlog/posts/1524285237604581 . April 18, 2017. Accessed September 4, 2017.

16. David D. 10 Things You Should Know About Goals. Forbes website. https://www.forbes.com/sites/daviddisalvo/2013/09/29/10-things-you-should-know-about-

goals/#66f747b7542c. September 29, 2013. Accessed August 29, 2017

ACKNOWLEDGMENTS

I would like to first express my gratitude to the main entity that inspired me to write this book. I never would have put pen to paper if not for the book "Published," by Chandler Bolt. "Published" brought out an entire book I never knew I had in me and made the process of self-publishing non-intimidating. If you're thinking about writing a book, I highly recommend it.

Thank you to my fiancé, Andrew, who insisted I keep going even when I was convinced that my book was horrid. You talked me off several ledges and made me believe that my writing was worth pursuing. I am ever grateful for you.

To the Poopfaces: Claire, Lauren, Mom, and Dad. Thank you for being excited about my book when I wasn't, and for your input, edits, and revisions that made my book way better. You guys are the bahst.

I would also like to thank Rachel Richards (hey, that's me!) for her beautiful artistic illustrations.

Disclaimer & Important Information

This book and its contents are for your personal use only and are protected by applicable copyright, patent, and trademark laws.

The information provided in this book is for general informational purposes only. It is not intended and under no circumstances should be construed as providing personal investment, tax, or legal advice or recommendations. The book also should not be construed as an offer to sell or the solicitation of an offer to buy, nor as a recommendation to buy, hold, or sell any security.

The author is not a registered investment advisor, a registered securities broker-dealer, or a certified financial planner, or otherwise licensed to give investment advice. All opinions, analyses, and information included herein are based on sources believed to be reliable, and the book has been written in good faith, but no representation or warranty of any kind, expressed or implied, is made, including but not limited to any representation or warranty concerning accuracy, completeness, correctness, timeliness, or appropriateness.

You are responsible for your own investment decisions, and each investor is solely responsible for analyzing and evaluating any information used or relied upon in making an investment decision. Before making any investment decision, you should thoroughly investigate the proposed investment, consider your personal situation, and consult with a qualified investment advisor. The information and opinions provided in this book should not be relied upon or used as a substitute for consultation with professional advisors.

The use of or reliance on the contents of this book is done solely at your own risk. No representation or warranty, expressed or implied, is made as to the accuracy, completeness, or correctness of this book's opinions, analyses, or information. Investment markets have inherent risks, there can be no guarantee of profits, and investors may lose money any time they invest in the stock market. Different types of investments involve varying degrees of risk, and there can be no assurance that any specific investment or strategy will be either suitable or profitable for a specific investment portfolio.

Past performance does not assure future returns. Therefore, no reader should assume that the performance of any investment approach discussed in this book will be profitable in the future, equal its past performance, or reach any performance objectives. The author shall have and accepts no liability of whatever nature in respect of any claims, damages, loss, or expense arising from or in connection with an investor's reliance on or use of this book.

In no event shall any reference to any third party or third-party product or service be construed as an approval or endorsement by the author. In particular, the author does not endorse or recommend the services of any particular broker, dealer, mutual fund company, or information provider.

The author may now or in the future have positions in or trade the securities discussed in the book.

URGENT PLEA!

Thank You For Reading My Book!

I appreciate all of your feedback and I love hearing what you have to say. I need your input to make the next version of this book and my future books better.

Please leave me a helpful review on Amazon letting me know what you thought of the book. Thanks so much!

-Rachel

Follow me on social media!

Facebook: www.facebook.com/moneyhoneyrachel

Instagram: @moneyhoneyrachel

Made in the USA
Lexington, KY
18 September 2017